Great Scenic Railways of
DEVON & CORNWALL

MICHAEL PEARSON

WAYZGOOSE

www.wayzgoose.org.uk Tel: 01283 713674 / 821472
Copyright: Michael Pearson All Rights Reserved
First Edition 2004 ISBN 0 9545383 6 6
Printed in Italy by STIGE, Via Pescarito 110, 10099 San Mauro

IN 1965 I spent a bedridden spring and early summer recuperating from meningitis, and my chief pastime was the compilation of a guide book and gazetteer to a county called Torshire, which my imagination had obligingly allowed me to bolt on to the seaward side of North Devon. The county town was known as Braunton Abbot and from it radiated a network of railway lines. For even at the age of twelve I understood the impact that the rival Great Western and London & South Western railways had made on the West Country, both in terms of moving about its mineral, maritime and agricultural wealth and of bringing vast numbers of holidaymakers to the region. With the self-indulgence of childhood I pictured myself the new S. P. B. Mais. Forty years on it felt like *deja vu* to be making a guide book for real, but at least it was refreshing to find the railways still moving goods and tourists, and that the West Country of my boyhood imagination was as Arcadian as I had always imagined it to be; give or take a retail park or two.

Freud would tell us these Devon and Cornwall railway byways appeal to us so much because they exist in a world where it is always holiday time. My own childhood holidays were taken in South Devon just as steam was gracefully giving way to diesel. In 1962 I encountered my first Great Western steam locomotive, *Lulworth Castle*, burnished and gleaming on a hot afternoon at Goodrington Sands. And later, bobbing about in the waves, watched *King Henry V* puffing towards Churston on a *Torbay Express* whose carriages were still painted chocolate & cream. At Plymouth I saw Bulleid Pacifics rubbing shoulders with Hawksworth Counties, and only felt short-changed when the Tavistock local came in behind the sort of Ivatt 2-6-2 tank I could see any day at home in the Midlands.

The following summer my parents unaccountably plumped for a boring beach on Italy's Adriatic Coast, and by 1964 only the Plymouth to Brighton express was still worked by steam. Nevertheless I discovered a growing affinity with the Western Region's idiosyncratic diesel hydraulic designs, the Hymeks and Westerns and Warships by then responsible for most of the West Country's trains. I even formed a sneaking regard for the pug-nosed little North British Type 2s which could just about be trusted to handle stopping trains and pick-up goods on the byways that had survived Beeching. But as I grew older against a background of railway retrenchment and regression, I began to grasp a greater awareness of the railway's role in the environment and its capacity to provide transport without necessarily compromising the landscape, rural or urban. In other words, it ceased to matter so much what was hauling me, as to where it was going. By then, though, I was too late to get to Bude, Sidmouth, Kingsbridge, Helston or Padstow by rail and I felt distinctly cheated, as though something of personal value had been stolen from me that I could never hope to re-acquire.

Twenty years later, I was reacquainted with the West Country. We had discovered a Cornish printer whose prices were well below those of his up-country competitors, and whose tolerant credit terms proved liberating to a small publisher whose stock was never likely to disappear off the shelves with the alacrity of a best-seller. It was good to be back, the railways seemed in rude health. Day-trips to Callington meant catching the overnight sleeper from Glasgow at Birmingham and transferring into an early HST at Temple Meads which would serve us a full cooked breakfast as we raced over the Somerset Levels. At Plymouth we decanted into an archaic diesel unit which wound its way up the Tamar Valley, passing so slowly through some of the cuttings that we could almost lean out and pick the primroses. On the way back we'd often be dropped at Liskeard, from where we would board a Class 50-hauled Paddington express, sinking gratefully into the well-sprung cushions of a compartment carriage in which a club-like atmosphere prevailed. In the confessional-like confines of a compartment you could make friends for life. Not in the sense that you subsequently swapped Christmas cards, but in that you would neither forget the strangers you met, nor the conversations you enjoyed.

Another twenty years on, it is gratifying to see the Great Scenic Railways of Devon & Cornwall still going strong: their significance recognised by a new generation of travellers, their role underwritten by partnerships between the rail industry and local bodies whose enthusiasms are infectious. Increased service patterns, refurbished and colourfully branded stations, jazz trains, rail ale trails and community events are rendering these railways more visible than they've been for a generation. Some of them may prove effective guinea pigs for a new era of Community Railways. The only way a village store can compete with the nearest out of town supermarket is for it to be dynamic, innovative and responsive to local demand. The same may be said of many a branch line railway. I hope this book encourages you to go and explore these lines and the beautiful landscapes and seascapes they serve. Change at Exeter for Arcady!

Michael Pearson

The Tarka Line

One of the Great Scenic Railways of Devon & Cornwall

THE TARKA LINE

wessextrains

Connecting People, Connecting Places

HENRY WILLIAMSON'S literary profile is disappointingly low these days. You won't find his prolific output well represented on the shelves of your local Waterstones or Ottakars. Only *Tarka the Otter* is widely available, and even that mostly finds itself pigeon-holed in the children's department. So it is good to see a writer, so demonstrably in harmony with the landscapes of the West Country, remembered in the naming of a scenic branch line, and particularly appropriate that the route follows closely the course of the River Taw where Tarka had so many of his adventures.

Branch line! It wasn't always thus. It may have been single track for much of its course, but fifty years ago the North Devon line resounded to the passage of the *Devon Belle* and the *Atlantic Coast Express* as post war holidaymakers headed in large numbers for Ilfracombe and the broad, windswept sands of the Atlantic Ocean. But, by the time the American travel writer Paul Theroux travelled along it in the summer of the Falklands War, finding it comically reminiscent of Bertie Wooster, the line had been rationalised into a sleepy backwater, an obvious candidate for closure in any ensuing round of cutbacks. In *The Kingdom By The Sea* (inadvertently one of the best railway travelogues ever compiled) he stoically accepts that it was soon to be swept away, a pessimism shared by Paul Atterbury when he came to write *End of the Line* a decade later.

Ironically, *The Tarka Line's* present status as a byway comes full circle back to its murky, mid 19th century origins as a *cause celebre* in the Battle of the Gauges. In those days it had acquired the dubious nickname 'Vicar of Bray Railway' after a 16th century Irish clergyman prone to changing his faith, if not his girth. The first section of the route between Exeter and Credition, constructed to the broad gauge and completed in 1847, bizarrely lay rusting for four whole years before agreement could be reached between waring factions lending their support to the broad and standard gauges with regard to the status and ownership of the route. Though built independently, it was naturally assumed that it would fall under the sphere of the Great Western Railway, and, indeed, the line through the Taw Valley to Barnstaple was completed to broad gauge dimensions in 1854. Then, controversially, by surreptitious if not fraudulent means, the rival London & South Western Railway acquired a controlling interest in the line and proceeded to lay an inner rail to permit standard gauge trains to work the route. Mixed gauge operations ensued for a number of years, the last broad gauge goods train reaching Credition in 1892.

Traditionally, trains for North Devon have usually originated at the old Southern Railway's 'Central' station, or 'Queen Street' as it had been known in earlier days. Often they would have come all the way from London Waterloo itself: huge long multi-portioned trains of green coloured coaching stock which would be frenetically divided and re-engined pending despatch to Okehampton, for Plymouth and North Cornwall, or Barnstaple for Ilfracombe or Bideford and Torrington. Today's short diesel units seem therefore lost in the lengthy platforms of Exeter Central; darting minnows where once there were imperious salmon.

What has not changed, however, is the ski-slope like descent from Central to St Davids, a 1 in 37 plunge from the purlieus of the hilltop cathedral city to the valley of the River Exe. You can still sense the caution with which the train is driven down to St Davids, passing through a short tunnel en route, wheels squealing in protestation at the sharp radius of the curve. In steam days the long expresses and heavy goods were banked up from St David's to Central, and the short connecting chord was often so busy that the bankers worked back down the incline attached to westbound passenger trains, three or four locomotives at a time.

ST DAVID'S was the Great Western station, and remains to this day a major stop on the line between Paddington and Penzance. In the heyday of competition between the Great Western and the Southern their services met each other in opposite directions at this point. For example, a Paddington to Plymouth express would pass southbound on the GWR's 'down' line through Exeter St David's and take the coastal route via Dawlish, whereas a Waterloo to Plymouth through train would head northwards on the 'up' line through St David's before branching off at Cowley Bridge Junction and reaching its destination via Okehampton. From Exeter to Plymouth via the Great Western line the mileage was (and, of course, remains) 52 miles. Surprisingly the Southern's long since severed route across the top of Dartmoor was a mere 7 miles longer. Rivalry was at its fiercest in the early 20th century as the two companies competed for the lucrative and prestigious Ocean Liner traffic in passengers and mail.

St David's station was originally opened in 1844 as the broad gauge terminus of the Bristol & Exeter Railway. On the edge of town in a neighbourhood once known as Red Cow Village. It is said that the city burghers frowned at anything so vulgar as a railway despoiling their ancient streets, though any engineer will tell you that the lie of the land was a more important factor. Brunel's initial buildings were rebuilt in 1864 by Henry Lloyd and Francis Fox and there were further changes made before the First World War rendering the station largely as you see it today. At one time it boasted a dining room. Gilbert Thomas* and his family sojourned there in May 1937 and between the roast chicken and the gooseberry tart filed out on to Platform 1 to watch the *Cornish Riviera* pass through hauled by *King Henry VII*. Prior to Beeching's savage pruning of the Southern's North Devon and North Cornwall routes it was a trainspotter's mecca, a resort for railfans *par excellence*, where on any given day dozens of differing locomotive designs might

*Double-Headed (David & Charles 1967)

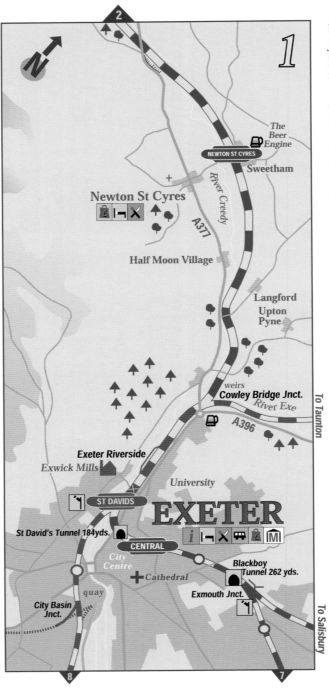

be admired. Picture them: Brylcreamed and duffle-bagged; jostling for pole-position at platform ends; munching Bowyers pork pies washed down with waxed cartons of vending machine milk; clutching Ian Allan ABCs and praying for an elusive 'cop'. Even in the diesel age St David's had its devotees, an enthusiastic following for the Western Region's idiosyncratic hydraulics, or later still, here to see the English Electric Class 50s swan-singing on the Waterloo trains. Now the angels are largely to be seen in the architecture, doubtless 'spinning in infinity' as Paul Simon sang on *Graceland*.

Swollen by passengers who have made connections from the main line at St David's, the Barnstaple diesel unit thrums its way northwards, paralleling the Exe. Riverside Yard is a pale shadow of its former self, filled now with forlorn ranks of stored rolling stock where once shunting and transfer workings were undertaken around the clock. Here, until finally lost to road transport in the 1960s, Cornwall's seasonal broccoli trains would pause to change crews and take water before proceeding north to Wales, the Midlands and London. In 1946 over 65,000 tons of Cornish broccoli went by rail, climaxing in nineteen special train-loads on 26th March. R. C. Riley gave an evocative account of this extraordinary traffic in the 1966 *Trains Annual*. In the July 1964 issue of *Modern Railways* it was reported that British Railways' Cornish agricultural traffic salesman grew every known variety of broccoli in his garden so as to be immediately on the scene as each kind ripened and was ready for transport.

COWLEY BRIDGE JUNCTION has long been a favoured haunt of railway photographers. Numerous published photographs depict classic scenes of 'West Country' Pacifics leaning into the curve off the North Devon line, or 'Castles' coming round the bend past the half-timbered gables of the Cowley Bridge Inn. Nowadays trains for Barnstaple (and Okehampton also on Summer Sundays) veer away from the main line on to single, jointed track which evokes a branch line flavour; prelude to an hour's journey into deepest Devon.

Some trains still call at NEWTON ST CYRES, which serves a sleepy hamlet and a railway-side pub brewing its own rail-themed ales. The timetable caters for those with a thirst for an evening or Sunday lunchtime in this tranquil location. Commuters use the much more frequent and handy bus service which serves the centre of Newton on the main road.

THE line climbs up to Crediton at 1 in 330, not unduly taxing the train. On the outskirts it passes 'Downes', historic home of General Sir Redvers Buller VC, something of a local hero, though also the first exponent of the concentration camp. Briefly, the track redoubles, and CREDITON station, the most important stop on the line, has the feel of a calling point of some consequence about it. A few of its buildings hark back to its origins as the terminus of the broad gauge line opened up from Exeter in the year of the Great Exhibition. Perhaps some of the local gentry set off from this very platform to journey to the Crystal Palace and marvel at the Wonders of the Empire. Archive photographs exist depicting the station in the Victorian period, by which time the line had become of mixed gauge. When, finally, the broad gauge was abandoned towards the end of the 19th century, the platforms were widened, leaving no hint now that the tracks once measured seven feet between the rails. One pleasing survival is the L&SWR company initials, carved in stone on the footbridge. The station building is now home to an extremely good tea room and craft shop, popular with locals and travellers alike.

A timber signal box overlooks a level crossing, and the signalman comes out to exchange tokens with the driver. Misleadingly it appears that the track remains double. Though, nowadays, the lines to Barnstaple and Okehampton are worked quite separately between Crediton and their parting of ways at what used to be known as Coleford Junction. At least the illusion of a trunk route remains, a timely reminder that you are journeying in the footsteps of express trains bound for North Devon, North Cornwall and Plymouth up until the 1960s.

The train slows for an ungated level-crossing at Salmon Pool. Milking herds graze lush farmland. One might easily imagine that farming hereabouts was a sinecure. If one didn't know better! The lucrative days of European farming subsidies and 'butter mountains' being long passed.

Skipping backwards and forwards across the river, the train reaches YEOFORD, originally a significant point of interchange between the Barnstaple and Okehampton lines. You wouldn't think it now! Alight here, and once the train has rattled away into the hills, the sounds are not of shunting but of the river plashing gently beneath the platform, all sense of activity long departed. At one time the down platform and adjoining bay boasted a refreshment room catering for passengers changing trains. The timber-built signal box

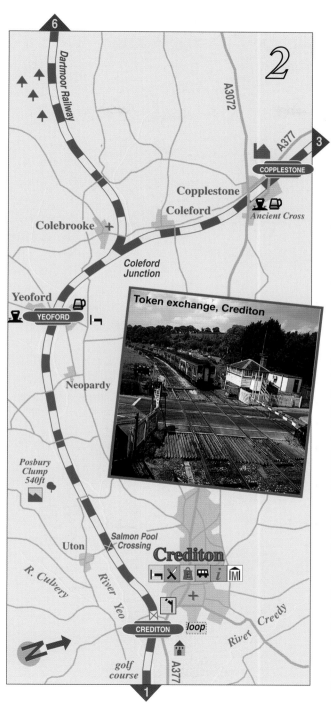

Token exchange, Crediton

contained a frame of 35 levers, and was raised to a lofty height on a brick base to enable the signalman to see clearly over the road bridge.

The hills grow taller, with sheep on their shoulders. Colebrook's handsome church tower watches over the bifurcation of the two railways. A long vanished signal box oversaw manoeuvres between the two double-tracked lines. Singling took place in 1971 following abandonment of regular services to Okehampton. It is difficult to grasp now just how busy this junction would have been prior to the rationalisation of the Southern lines in Devon and Cornwall. Something in the region of eighty trains a day would have passed Coleford Junction in the summer months; all round the clock: expresses, stopping trains, newspapers and parcels, goods, perishables, ballast.

The North Devon line was double as far as COPPLESTONE, the first station on the Barnstaple line, which sets the architectural tone for the rest of the journey. Just before you get there you pass the summit of the line, 350 feet above sea level. Work commenced on doubling the whole route through to Barnstaple in 1906. During the middle years of the 20th century, when the line was stretched to its capacity, completion of this scheme would have been welcomed. In 1910, however, the London & South Western signed a pact with the Great Western to effectively pool the resources of their competing routes to Barnstaple, and the doubling got no further than bridge widening, evidence of which is still plainly visible where the line spans rivers or passes beneath roads. In the event, the GWR took steps to improve their route from Taunton to Barnstaple in the 1930s, as the Southern slumbered unconcernedly on.

Though all the intermediate stations had crossing loops, many of them were too short to accommodate the growing length of trains. When passing took place, it was often necessary to shunt one train into a siding, hardly a practice commensurate with tight scheduling. According to Volume 1 of David & Charles's seminal work *A Regional History of the Railways of Great Britain*, as late as 1957 the Southern Region were promising to lengthen the loops and introduce centralized traffic control. But within five years the Western Region had taken over all the old Southern lines in Devon and Cornwall, and its management team were taking a vindictive delight in closing or curtailing the routes of their historic, and manifestly still bitterly regarded rival.

CROSSING the confusing watershed between a river called the Yeo which flows southwards to join the Creedy, and a river called the Yeo which flows northwards to join the Taw, the railway steadily descends from its summit, becoming acquainted with the A377 which will accompany it for much of the way to Barnstaple. Rolling countryside defines this undemonstrative heart of Devon where, by and large, what settlements there are, cling to the upper slopes of the hills, marked for miles ahead by lofty church towers. Railway mileposts, stranded in the widened bed of the second track that never got laid, tick off the miles from London Waterloo, as if they still trust implicitly that your train will have commenced its journey on the south bank of the Thames. Such is the family resemblance of MORCHARD ROAD to Copplestone, you're half left believing you've nodded off in the soporific countryside, and not made any forward progress at all.

The train coasts down into LAPFORD on a gradient of 1 in 145, and crosses the Yeo a couple of times. You catch a glimpse (on the right) of a fine old mill building which retains its weatherboarded luccam. But it is the more substantial industrial premises to the left which deserve fuller attention. This was a creamery, opened in 1928, where the famous tinned Ambrosia Creamed Rice was once manufactured in huge quantities, creating considerable traffic for the railway, both in terms of raw material inward such as coal and milk, and finished products out. The works closed in 1970 as production was transferred to more modern premises at Lifton but, as you can see, most of the buildings remain, in light industrial use. Fertilizer was shipped by rail until 1993, the last use by freight of *The Tarka Line*.

Looking at the creamwashed station now - typically, in domestic use - it is difficult to appreciate the former layout, made curious by the fact that the down platform stood to the south of the road bridge, islanded by the loop but fenced off from up trains. The loop remains intact, but rarely used, having last been required for the running-round of fertilizer trains in the early Nineties.

Bulleid's West Country Pacific, 34102 *Lapford*, remained, along with 34023 *Blackmore Vale*, the last of his unrebuilt 'air-smoothed' locomotives in regular use up until the end of steam on the Southern Region in 1967. Unfortunately, unlike *Blackmore Vale*, it did not survive into preservation, though an unnaturally high proportion of his locomotives did, courtesy of the famous Barry scrapyard in South Wales, where over two hundred steam locomotives escaped the cutter's torch for long enough for their true value to posterity to be recognised.

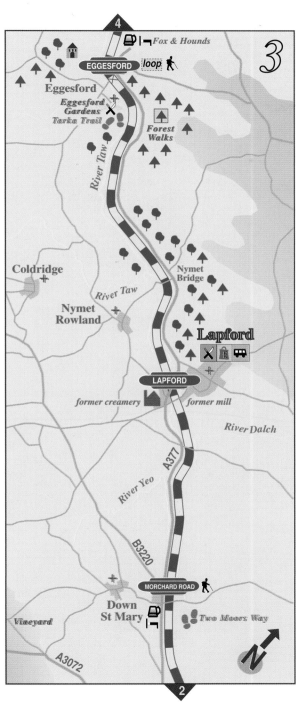

Lovelier and lovelier grows the journey as the train swoops down through woodland into the valley of the Taw. The river's source lies up on Dartmoor in a sponge-like wilderness of peat which also spawns the Teign and the Tavy and the Dart. Henry Williamson wrote poetically of the Taw's beginnings in Chapter 11 of *Tarka the Otter*, describing 'the faint cry of a river new-born': 'its first cascade' and 'its first bubbles'; and how it 'ran strong and bright over its bed of granite... glinting and singing'.

By the time the Taw is joined by the Yeo near Nymet Rowland it has grown into a river with a tradition for salmon and sea trout fishing. Regrettably, from the angler's point of view, the Taw has declined as a fishery during the last half century, though it remains the most productive in the West Country. In recent years it has only been by the buying-out of netting rights in the estuary that sufficient numbers of fish have remained capable of reaching their spawning grounds upstream. The rod-fishing season starts at the beginning of March and continues through to the end of September. Any salmon caught, however, must be returned into the river until mid-June. There are hotels, well-known amongst the fishing fraternity, that have beats on the Taw at Eggesford and Umberleigh, though one doubts if tweeded, dry-fly fishermen, still arrive by train.

If fishing in the Taw Valley (which in the guise of Bulleid's rebuilt Pacific 34027 is one of the best known locomotives on the preserved steam circuit) sets you in mind of Scotland, the conifer plantations only serve to exaggerate the illusion. It is interesting to discover that it was in the neighbourhood of Eggesford that the Forestry Commission first began the sometimes controversial practice of planting coniferous trees in large masses in 1919, having acquired the land from the Earl of Portsmouth's estate which had been broken up just prior to the First World War. For many years the Earl's magnificent 19th century mansion on the hillside above Eggesford station had been a romantically decaying ruin, but recently it has been partially restored.

Nowadays EGGESFORD station is the only passing point on the Tarka Line between Crediton and Barnstaple. The train crew go through a series of arcane procedures to operate the level-crossing barriers and effect a change of token. Such rituals are all part and parcel of the rural railway's appeal, even to travellers who have no real interest in trains. There was once a comparatively busy goods yard here, with an oil depot, an auction mart and an abattoir, and, doubtless, a brisk trade in the despatch of freshly caught salmon!

THE Little Dart flows down to join the Taw under the hilltop town of Chumleigh, the most substantial settlement in the neighbourhood which inexplicably never had a station to call its own. Perhaps this explains why it remained a sleepy sort of place, and didn't grow, for example, to the size of Crediton. Paradoxically, now that the railway is no longer of paramount importance to the local economy, Chumleigh has acquired more significance; more facilities than can be found in many a mile, a frequent bus service from Crediton and the main school for a large hinterland.

Cattle and sheep graze in lush meadows beside the river. Henry Williamson referred poetically to these meadows being made of 'age-long silt filling the valley's groin' and the river, viewed from the hilltops, 'like a viper broken by a buzzard's beak and claws'. Red soil, freshly ploughed, provides variety of colour in amongst a kaleidoscope of green. The woods are too dense to allow you a glimpse of Colleton Manor dating from 1612, and the train too swift to see anything other than a blur of Colleton Mills.

With most of the villages located snugly in the hills, whilst the railway was built along the Taw Valley, it was inevitable that some hefty distances accrued between the stations and the places they were somewhat loosely named after. KINGS NYMPTON is a good example, a three mile walk from its namesake, and some four hundred feet lower. But, even more incredibly, the station was originally named South Molton Road, a rather tenuous link, even by Victorian railway standards, with a town nine miles to the north-east, far better served by the Great Western Railway's Taunton to Barnstaple line. The name was changed in 1951, by which time traffic was ebbing away from this remote station, once made busy by the monthly cattle market held at Fortescue Cross.

Road, and river swap sides, but the railway remains in the middle, happy to remain shoulder to shoulder with its two companions. Junction Pool is the confluence of the Taw with its tributary the Mole, which flows down off Darlick Moors on the southern flank of Exmoor. Tarka fought with a one-eyed eel in this Junction Pool, but it is in the pages of Williamson's *Salar the Salmon* that the setting is brought more vividly to life. In this now arguably less well-known book, first published in 1935 (eight years after *Tarka the Otter*) and dedicated to T. E. Lawrence, Chapter 10 is entitled 'Junction Pool'. It elaborates on the building of the railway and how the cylindrical piers of the

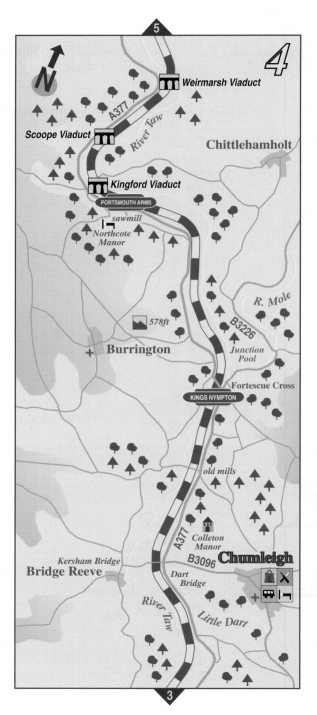

railway bridge caused the Taw, in its winter spates, to scoop out the gravel from its bed and deposit it below the confluence of the Mole, thus forming the basis of an islet soon colonised by vegetation. Williamson, it is widely acknowledged, took pains to maximise verisimilitude, *Tarka* was rewritten seventeen times. However, in *Tarka* he describes the railway bridges of the North Devon line being built of stone with iron girders, correcting this more accurately to steel in *Salar*. But it is churlish and pedantic to draw attention to such inaccuracies against the achievement of his nature writings, timeless classics which deserve a wider audience than literary fashion now allows.

Debilitated and disillusioned by his experiences in the First World War, Henry Williamson arrived in North Devon - heralded solely by the roar of his Norton motorcycle - in 1921, renting a cottage at Georgeham, to the north-west of Braunton, for one shilling and sixpence a week. He occupied the house hermit style along with a menagerie of dogs, cats, birds (especially owls) and an otter cub which he had helped rescue after its mother had been shot. *Tarka the Otter* was inspired by his relationship with this cub, and though he had published several novels before it appeared, it made his reputation, winning the Hawthornden Prize of 1928. The following year, married now and with a young son, he moved to Shallowford, on the banks of the River Bray (a tributary of the Mole) and began to gather material together for a book in the *Tarka* vein concerning the life of a salmon.

Except for a period during the Second World War when he farmed at Stiffkey on the North Norfolk Coast, Williamson spent the rest of his often abrasive life in North Devon. Divorced twice, he also fathered a child by Ann Thomas, daughter of the poet Edward. Lawrence of Arabia was a close friend. Fellow motor-cycle enthusiasts, Lawrence was returning from despatching a telegram to Williamson, arranging that he should visit him a day or two later, in Dorset, when he met an untimely death on his own machine. During the Thirties Henry Williamson flirted with Oswald Mosley's brand of fascism. He died in 1977, coincidentally as the film version of *Tarka the Otter* was being made. He is buried in Georgeham, accessible by bus from Barnstaple, for those inspired by the *Tarka Line* and inclined towards a pilgrimage.

PORTSMOUTH ARMS derived its name from a neighbouring inn. The Taw widens as the valley bottoms out, the characteristic flat-decked bridges now afforded the status of viaducts and bestowed with names.

BARNSTAPLE

Course of Lynton & Barnstaple Railway

Course of Barnstaple & Taunton Railway (GWR)

A39

Town Centre

i

BARNSTAPLE

Tarka Trail

River Taw

Tarka Trail

A361

Course of Barnstaple & Ilfracombe Railway (SR)

Course of Barnstaple & Torrington Railway (SR)

A39

Taw Viaduct

folly

Tawstock

school

Week

Bishop's Tawton

Codden Hill 630ft

New Bridge

Black Viaduct

CHAPELTON

sawmill

UMBERLEIGH

River Taw

Umberleigh

UMBERLEIGH

A377

Fishleigh Farmhouse

Atherington

UMBERLEIGH may have lost its up platform, its cattle pens and its signal box, but it retains a Southern Railway concrete 'running-in' nameboard, evoking much nostalgia. Theroux considered it a likely setting for *Jeeves Lays an Egg*, but in the context of these Taw Valley wayside stations, it is a significant railhead, and like Eggesford, a centre for fishing. Beyond here, the line actually did get doubled, in the late 19th century; a status it retained until 1971.

Atherington's distinguished church is prominent to the west as the railway crosses the Taw once again. The line is less prone to curvature now as the valley widens.

CHAPELTON, a private dwelling, is one of the best maintained stations, whitewashed and proudly displaying a green 'Southern' nameboard. The neighbouring sawmill once relied heavily on the railway for transport.

Under Codden Hill the line runs down to Barnstaple. Bishop's Tawton church has a crocketed spire, unusual in this part of Devon. In parkland across the river stands Tawstock Court, with its prominent stuccoed Gothick frontage, now a school. The adjoining church of St Peter's is notable for its carving of a Hinky Punk, a two-legged beast said to lure travellers into swamps, and possibly the source of the expression 'hanky panky'.

Regular travellers, sensing journey's end, gather their chattels. Not that long ago, in respective portions of the *Atlantic Coast Express*, you could have travelled on beside the estuaries of the Taw and Torridge to Bideford and Torrington, or over the hills to the seaside resort of Ilfracombe on the North Devon coast. At its zenith, Barnstaple's railway network totalled no less than five routes, the line you are travelling upon being the sole survivor.

What has been abandoned? The Great Western Railway's line from Norton Fitzwarren on the outskirts of Taunton, closed in 1966; the Southern Railway routes to Torrington and Ilfracombe already mentioned above, closed to passenger trains in 1965 and 1970 respectively; and, perhaps most heartbreakingly of all, the lovely Lynton & Barnstaple narrow gauge railway, a victim of Southern Railway indifference in 1935, one of the most mourned railway closures of all time.

Ilfracombe's hoteliers were particularly upset at British Rail's post-Beeching decision to close their line, perceiving that traffic had been none too subtly discouraged by poor timetabling. There were brief hopes that the route could be operated privately. Similarly there were suggestions that Bideford might have its passenger services reintroduced in the early Eighties, the track still being used by clay trains. Neither took place, but a group *is* slowly and painstakingly restoring the Lynton & Barnstaple, a short section of the line

already having been relaid in the vicinity of Woody Bay.

One final viaduct spans the Taw as the train slows for BARNSTAPLE. A ring road and electricity pylons signify the periphery of a modern town, aided and abetted by the inevitable retail park with DIY outlets and fast food joints. An abandoned railway bridge, now used by pedestrians and cyclists, marks the course of a loop laid from the GWR station at Victoria Road to facilitate through running to and from Ilfracombe. The station in use at Barnstaple now - 'Barum' in the archaic vernacular - was formerly known as Barnstaple Junction. Barnstaple Town lay across the Taw, much better positioned for the town centre. Still in situ, it has become a community centre, sporting 'Southern' green signs; though the curving iron bridge which carried trains across the river has entirely vanished. The ring road occupies the course of the Great Western line, but the platform edge remains, as does the goods shed, appropriated by a wine merchant.

You can enjoy the topography of the Torrington and Ilfracombe lines by hiring a bicycle at Barnstaple station and pedalling along the *Tarka Trail*. With a little imagination the past is rediscoverable. No longer a staid adult, embroiled in nebulous 21st century employment, you are on the footplate of a Maunsell Mogul, steaming freely down to Torrington with milk empties ...

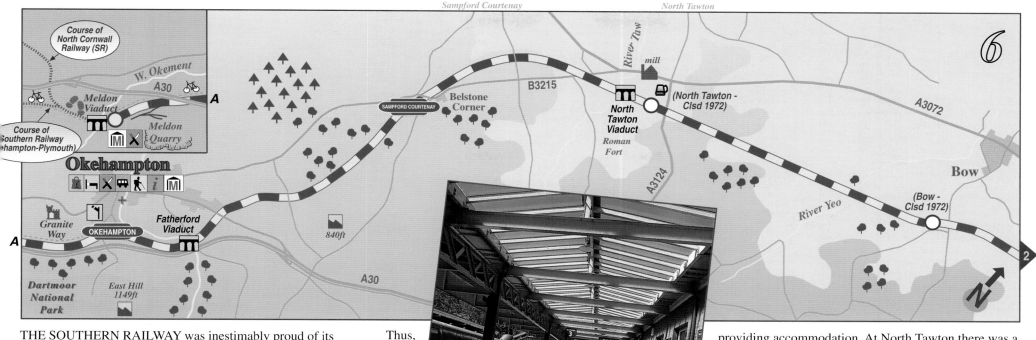

THE SOUTHERN RAILWAY was inestimably proud of its Dartmoor Main Line: 'Probably the finest panorama of England obtainable from any railway carriage window ...' to quote their publicity material. Long ago lost as a through route, you can at least travel as far as Okehampton on Summer Sundays aboard Wessex Trains diesel units sponsored by Devon County Council. And having reached Okehampton you can hire bicycles and pedal along the Granite Way which follows the course of the old line more or less as far as Lydford.

When the last scheduled passenger train rolled dolefully out of Okehampton for Exeter in 1972, you would have needed to be of an optimistic disposition to envisage ever being able to reach that pretty market town on the northern edge of Dartmoor ever again by rail. Fortunately the track had to be kept in place to carry ballast trains from Meldon Quarry - as many as five each day in the 1980s. In 1994 the quarry and the line up from Coleford Junction fell into private ownership, and within a short time with local authority encouragement and support Okehampton's crumbling station was being splendidly and sympathetically refurbished as a visitor centre and railhead for Dartmoor.

Thus, once a week in the summer months, trains set off from Exeter in the footsteps of the Southern's Plymouth expresses of old, diverging from the Barnstaple Line at what used to be known as Coleford Junction (Map 2) and making their way round the northern skirts of Dartmoor. It is a journey difficult to resist, a journey full of railway ghosts. The fact that branches brush the carriage sides emphasises the infrequency of services, and even the modern diesel unit knows that it has its work cut out to make the ascent, after all, the summit of the line just west of Meldon viaduct lay the best part of a thousand feet above sea level, a sea level left less than thirty miles behind at Exeter.

The old station buildings at Bow and North Tawton are in domestic use now, but it's good to see their handsome architecture has survived. Even the goods shed at Bow is

providing accommodation. At North Tawton there was a brisk trade in rabbits and wool, the latter originating from a substantial mill still visible from the line. Hereabouts you catch your first glimpses of Dartmoor from the left hand side of the train; though frustrating levels of vegetation, allowed to flourish since the demise of steam, do mask some of the views that earlier railway travellers would have enjoyed.

Sampford Courtenay station re-opened on 21st May 2004. It should prove a useful halt for walkers. A few minutes later you reach OKEHAMPTON, where the opportunity offers itself to change into the 'Dartmoor Pony' train for the short run to Meldon, to catch one of several bus services serving Dartmoor, or to just enjoy the facilities of the charmingly refurbished station with its cafeteria and excellent model railway shop. Alternatively, you can 'play trains' by bike, picturing yourself a Bulleid 'West Country' Pacific, climbing the 1 in 77 to Meldon, climaxed with a crossing of the famous wrought-iron viaduct erected in 1874 to carry the railway across the deep gorge of the West Okement River. Apply the brakes and savour the view from a hundred and thirty feet up. With Yes Tor on the south-eastern horizon all seems pretty much right with the world.

13

Gazetteer

Barnstaple
Map 5

The advent of the railways hastened the demise of Barnstaple as a port. Silted up now, you cross into town over a Taw disappointingly bereft of shipping upon a handsome medieval bridge infuriatingly filled with traffic. Less railways, no shipping; draw your own conclusions. But traffic problems notwithstanding, 'Barum's' streets have a spacious feel to them and this is a nice town to saunter in, picking up clues to a perhaps more colourful past when gloves and lace and pottery were amongst the staple trades. A handsome Victorian furniture factory overlooks the station end of the river bridge, lending somewhat more dignity to the scene than the adjacent retail park.

Accommodation
ROYAL & FORTESCUE - Boutport Street (town centre, 10 minutes walk from the station). Tel: 01271 342289 *www.royalfortescue.co.uk* Comfortable town centre hotel with three star rating.
THE IMPERIAL - Taw Vale Parade. Tel: 01271 345861 *www.brend-hotels.co.uk* Four star hotel commanding fine river views.

Eating & Drinking
62 THE BANK - Boutport Street. Tel: 01271 324446. Cafe bar and bistro adjoining the Royal & Fortescue.
GIOVANNI'S - Boutport Street. Tel: 01271 321274. Italian.
PAINTED FAN - Holland Street. Tel: 01271 375888. Chinese restaurant opposite the old electricity works.
ROLLE QUAY INN - Rolle Street. Tel: 01271 345182. Town pub overlooking yet another river called the Yeo. Easy access via Tarka Trail.

Shopping
Head for the PANNIER MARKET and BUTCHERS ROW and you won't be disappointed. The former is a thriving indoor market deriving its name from the traditional habit of farm-folk selling their wares from 'panniers' or baskets. The latter is a handsome, one-sided street of delicatessens, fishmongers and butchers shops selling the best of North Devon produce. Occupying the site of the former goods yard and engine shed, BRIAN FORD is purportedly the UK's largest independent food retailer.

Things to Do
TOURIST INFORMATION - The Square (turn right over Long Bridge) Tel: 01271 375000 *www.northdevon.com*
MUSEUM OF BARNSTAPLE & NORTH DEVON - The Square. Tel: 01271 346747. Open Mon-Sat, 9.30am-5pm. Excellent displays of local history for free!
BARNSTAPLE HERITAGE CENTRE - Riverfront. Tel: 01271 373003. Lively recreations of Barnstaple's vivid past. Open daily from 10am, small entrance charge. Gift shop.
LYNTON & BARNSTAPLE RAILWAY - Woody Bay, 16 miles north-east of Barnstaple, connecting buses. Tel: 01598 763487. Revival of the much lamented narrow gauge railway gathers pace.

Walking & Cycling
Former railway lines have been resurfaced and named the TARKA TRAIL to provide 33 miles of traffic free walking and cycling. Handily placed at Barnstaple railway station, Tarka Trail Cycle Hire offer immediate access to these admirable routes. Open daily from mid March to early November - Tel: 01271 324202. Bike hire is also available from Fremington Quay (where Southern Railway engine coal used to be brought in by sea) 3 miles west of Barnstaple - Tel: 01271 372586 *www.biketrail.co.uk*

Connections
TAXIS - A1 Taxis, Tel: 01271 322922.
BUSES - good connections to the former haunts of the *Atlantic Coast Express*. Service 30 runs hourly (Mon-Sat) direct from Barnstaple railway station to Ilfracombe, other services depart from the bus station in the town centre. Tel: 0870 608 2 608.

Chapelton
Map 5

Remote and not particularly well served, Chapelton station offers theoretical access to the splendid FISHLEIGH FARMHOUSE FOODS shop specialising in North Devon foods and drinks open daily except for Mondays. On Friday and Saturday evenings it transforms itself into the BLUE RIVER RESTAURANT. Mouth-watering stuff - Tel: 01769 560242.

Copplestone
Map 2

All but ignored by the illustrious *Shell Guides* of the past, Copplestone hosts a 10th century granite pillar ten feet high, transported from Dartmoor around 905 as a memorial to Bishop Putta, set upon and done to death whilst on his way between Crediton and North Tawton. Ernest Bevin lived in the village for five years from 1889, prior to his mercurial rise from farm labourer to Foreign Secretary by 1945. New housing may persuade the SRA as to the wisdom of an increase in service frequency. Facilities include a well-stocked post office stores, together with a pub called THE CROSS - Tel: 01363 84273 - offering bar food at lunchtimes and in the evenings.

Crediton
Map 2

A saint and a soldier constitute this amiable mid-Devon town's most famous sons. The missionary St Boniface was born here in 680; Redvers Buller, hero of the Zulu and Boer wars, in 1839. In between Crediton - which derives its name from the River Creedy - made and lost a fortune in the wool trade and claimed, then lost, the Bishopric of Devon. The magnificence of the parish church reflects this former ecclesiastical status.

Accommodation
GREAT PARK FARM - Tel: 01363 772050. Farmhouse bed & breakfast beside the railway.

Eating & Drinking
STATION TEA ROOMS - railway station. Tel: 01363 777766. Shining example of station catering on a par with Lady Foley's, Great Malvern.

Delicious light meals, crafts and interesting displays of local railway history.

Shopping
Lively Farmers Market on the first Saturday of the month. Excellent delicatessen called TRELOAR'S in the High Street - Tel: 01363 772332.

Things to Do
TOURIST INFORMATION - High Street. Tel: 01363 772006 *www.middevon.gov.uk/tourism*
DOWNES - on A377 half a mile east of the station. Tel: 01363 439046. Palladian mansion and gardens open Mondays and Tuesdays from mid-April to early July. Guided tours.

Walking
TownTrail leaflet available from the TIC.

Connections
TAXIS - Carey's Cars, Tel: 01363 777714.
BUSES - service 347 provides a useful cross-country link with Tiverton. Tel: 0870 608 2 608.

Eggesford
Map 3

Idyllic, scattered settlement on the banks of the Taw. The church is beautifully situated in splendid isolation on the hillside above the river and the railway. It contains particularly fine monuments - when open!

Accommodation, Eating & Drinking
FOX & HOUNDS COUNTRY HOTEL - 3 minutes walk from station. Tel: 01769 580345 *www.foxandhoundshotel.co.uk* Very comfortable 'fishing' hotel offering good value accommodation, plus bar and restaurant food open to non-residents. Features in the Tarka Line Rail Ale Trail leaflet.

Things to Do
EGGESFORD GARDENS - 10 minutes walk to south-west of station. Enterprising garden centre, plus gifts and crafts and clothing. Tel: 01769 580250. Open daily 9.30am to 5pm. Good 'garden' restaurant.

Walking
Forest walks and TARKA TRAIL.

Exeter
Maps 1, 7 & 8

It is a mistake to construe Exeter simply as a gateway to Devon and Cornwall. By rights it ought to be up there with York and Bath and Stratford-on-Avon in terms of tourism. Make it your business to buck the trend. Visit Northernhay and Rougemont Gardens, the Cathedral and the Quay and you will be more than pleasantly surprised.

Accommodation, Eating & Drinking
GREAT WESTERN HOTEL - St David's Station Approach. Tel: 01392 274039. *www.greatwesternhotel.com* 2 star hotel beside St David's station. Restaurant and bar open to non-residents, the latter hosting a particularly wide range of real ales, an admirable resort for real ale connoisseurs with time between trains.
HOTEL BARCELONA - Magdelan Road. Tel: 01392 281000 *www.hotelbarcelona-uk.com* Vibrant conversion of former eye infirmary. Nearest station - St Thomas.

RAFFLES HOTEL - Blackall Road. Tel: 01392 270200. Victorian town house, emphasis on organic food. Nearest station - Central.
BENDENE HOTEL - Richmond Road. Tel: 01392 213526 www.bendene.co.uk Well-appointed yet inexpensive accommodation with outdoor swimming pool close to city centre. Nearest station - Central.
YHA - Countess Wear Road. Tel: 0870 770 5826. Budget priced hostel accommodation.
ROYAL CLARENCE - Cathedral Yard. Tel: 01392 319955. One of England's oldest hotels in prime setting by the cathedral. Includes Michael Caines' celebrated bar/restaurant - Tel: 01392 310031 www.michaelcaines.com.
AL-FARID - Cathedral Yard. Tel: 01392 494444 www.havagoodtime.co.uk Moroccan tapas bar and restaurant.
RED SQUARE - Castle Street. Tel: 01392 411292 www.redsquarerestaurant.co.uk Authentic Russian cuisine.
CARVED ANGEL CAFE - Cathedral Yard. Tel: 01392 210303. Stylish modern cafe/restaurant offering fine views of cathedral close. www.carvedangel.com

Shopping
Every Thursday there's a Farmers Market on Eastgate, a good opportunity to obtain local Devon produce. Down on the picturesque Quayside you'll encounter some excellent craft and antique outlets. Gandy Street (near Central Station) is a quaint cobbled street hosting a variety of independent and specialist outlets.

Things to Do
TOURIST INFORMATION - Civic Centre, Paris Street. Tel: 01392 265700 www.exeter.gov.uk
QUAY HOUSE VISITOR CENTRE - The Quay. Tel: 01392 271611. Audio-visual displays of the city's two thousand year history. Open daily April to October, weekends in winter.
RED COAT GUIDES - an ideal way to learn about the city from a loquacious local. Tel: 01392 265203.
ROYAL ALBERT MEMORIAL MUSEUM - Queen Street. Tel: 01392 665858. Open daily (ex Sunday) a fine provincial museum and art gallery just yards from Central Station.
UNDERGROUND PASSAGES - Romangate Passage (off High Street). Tel: 01392 665887. Explore 14th century subterranean water supply channels. Not suitable for claustrophobics!
BOAT TRIPS - cruises along the Exeter Ship Canal. Tel: 07984 368442 or 07831 108319.

Walking & Cycling
Self-guided WOOLLEN TRAIL leaflets provide a dual opportunity to explore the city on foot and delve into the history of its most important medieval industry. The EXETER SHIP CANAL offers excellent off-road walking and cycling along its towpath. Bicycle and canoe hire is available from Saddles & Paddles at Kings Wharf - Tel: 01392 424241 www.saddlepaddle.co.uk

Connections
TAXIS - Capital Taxis, Tel: 01392 433433.
BUSES - Tel: 01392 427711.
CAR HIRE - Abbeyford Car Hire, Tel: 01392 214242 www.abbeyfordcarhire.co.uk

Kings Nympton   Map 4
Lovely name, little to do!

Lapford   Map 3
Hilltop village with creamy connotations, a splendid church, and a belt of housing added when the rice pudding factory was in its prime.

Eating & Drinking
YEO VALE INN - adjacent railway station. Tel: 01363 83844. Features in the Tarka Line Rail Ale Trail leaflet. Teign Valley beers, food and skittle alley.
OLD MALT SCOOP INN - village centre. Tel: 01363 83330. 'Everything a village pub should be' according to the Good Beer Guide. Bar and restaurant food (except on Mondays!). Sharps Doom Bar bitter and guest ales.

Shopping
SPAR shop at garage near station and post office with cash machine in village centre, quarter of an hour's walk uphill.

Morchard Road   Map 3
Railhead for the delightfully named but distant villages of Zeal Monachorum, Down St Mary and Morchard Bishop. The DEVONSHIRE DUMPLING - Tel: 01363 85102 - is a cosy pub offering food and bed & breakfast adjacent to the station. There is a vineyard at Down St Mary - Tel: 01363 82300 www.english-vineyard.co.uk

Newton St Cyres   Map 1
Pretty village short-changed by the main road - if only it was centred more on the comparative calm of the railway! The parish church of St Cyr & St Julitta is nevertheless well worth the walk. The BEER ENGINE - Tel: 01392 851282 - beside the station is a CAMRA recommended brew-pub blissfully free from any noise other than the hubbub of its customers. Excellent home made food and a railway theme to its beers, such as Piston Bitter and Sleeper Heavy. Recommended! Bed & breakfast available at the Glebe House - Tel: 01392 851353. Post office stores and another pub in the village centre.

Okehampton   Map 6
Charmingly unostentatious market town on the northern edge of Dartmoor and a good base for exploring that uniquely dramatic wilderness. The parish church of St James is mostly Victorian having been rebuilt in 1842 following a fire - it boasts windows by William Morris. Okehampton Castle is a romantic ruin.

Accommodation
YHA - Klondyke Road (adjacent railway station). Tel: 01837 53916. Budget-price hostel accommodation in a former railway goods shed!
WHITE HART HOTEL - Fore Street. Tel: 01837 52730. Two star hotel in town centre, 10 minutes downhill walk from the station.

Eating & Drinking
BULLEID BUFFET - snacks and light meals in a railway cafeteria environment named after the incomparable (if eccentric) locomotive engineer. Restaurant car dining on certain dates - Tel: 01837 55667.

Shopping
Good selection of shops in the town centre. 'Pannier' market on Saturdays. Well stocked model railway/gift shop on the station.

Things to Do
TOURIST INFORMATION - West Street. Tel: 01837 53020 www.discoverdartmoor.com
DARTMOOR RAILWAY - Tel: 01837 55667. Charmingly refurbished railway station recalling the great days of the Southern Railway. Short train rides to Meldon and Sampford Courtenay.
OKEHAMPTON CASTLE - Tel: 01837 52844. Medieval home of the Earls of Devon. Open April to October under the aegis of English Heritage.

Walking & Cycling
The GRANITE WAY offers eleven miles of off-road walking and cycling along the former route of the Southern Railway's highly scenic Okehampton to Tavistock main line, including the opportunity to cross the majestic Meldon Viaduct, 120 feet above the West Okement River. Cycle hire obtainable from the Dartmoor Railway or the YHA. Local rambling leaflets are also available for the area.

Connections
TAXIS -Okehampton Taxis, Tel: 01837 52421.
BUSES - useful connecting services to places such as Exeter (except in the case of Summer Sundays) Tavistock and Bude no longer served by rail. Tel: 0870 608 2 608. Additionally, there are excellent opportunities on Summer Sundays to explore Dartmoor by bus, including a hugely nostalgic vintage bus service linking Okehampton station with Rosemoor Gardens near Torrington.

Portsmouth Arms   Map 4
Remote platform serving eponymous inn: THE PORTSMOUTH ARMS - Tel: 01769 561117. Also close at hand is NORTHCOTE MANOR, a country house hotel and restaurant - Tel: 01769 560501 www.northcote-manor.co.uk

Umberleigh   Map 5
Small community on the banks of the Taw. The RISING SUN is a noted fishermen's hotel open to non-residents for bar and restaurant food. Tel: 01769 560447. Small PO by the station.

Yeoford   Map 2
Dreamy village on the River Yeo. The MARE & FOAL - Tel: 01363 84348 - stands just down the road from the station and features in the Tarka Rail Ale Trail. Close by WARRENS FARM offers accommodation in a charming 16th century Devon longhouse - Tel: 01363 84304. NORTH DOWN FARM is a visitor centre for rare breeds and rural life - Tel: 01363 84289 www.northdownfarm.com

IT is no coincidence that the Exeter to Exmouth line shares the image of its logo with the Royal Society for the Protection of Birds. The estuary of the River Exe, along which the railway runs for the majority of its length, is one of England's most outstanding habitats for birds, rendering your train an effective mobile hide as it trundles down the line between Topsham and Exmouth. The avocet is a wading bird which winters on the Exe estuary, sometimes in numbers exceeding five hundred birds. Long-legged and distinctively coloured in black and white stripes, it can also be recognised by a long, upwardly curving bill designed for sweeping shallow water in search of shrimps. The name derives from the French for judge on account of the similarity in colour of plumage.

The Exeter & Exmouth Railway opened in 1861. When first promoted, a few years earlier, it had been planned to build it to broad gauge dimensions as a branch of the South Devon Railway, but the machiavellian London & South Western again managed to acquire a dominating interest in the line, as they had done with the North Devon. You can reflect on the dynamics of railway history as you settle back in the comfort of your modern diesel unit, climbing the formidable 1 in 37 gradient out of St David's and up to Exeter Central. A short tunnel - which in its day must have resounded to the bark of the bankers whose job it was to push heavily loaded trains up the hill - filters out any residual Great Western atmosphere, and by the time you pull into 'Central' there's a very real feeling of being in 'Southern' territory.

Up until 1933 EXETER CENTRAL had been known as Exeter Queen Street; a station 'as dark as a crypt' according to David St John Thomas, or 'queer, draughty and scruffy' in the words of T.W.E. Roche. Growing volumes of traffic necessitated a radical reconstruction, and the Southern Railway came up with a pleasing design that was both practical to operate and easy on the eye. Two lengthy through platforms were provided to facilitate the marshalling of trains, for the Southern favoured the use of portions, and the long Waterloo to West of England expresses would be divided into Plymouth, North Cornwall and North Devon sections here, with, in the majority of cases, restaurant and dining cars being uncoupled too. The procedure would take place in reverse for up, eastbound trains.

It must have been entertaining for even the most disinterested onlooker to be on Central station in the Fifties, watching as the various portions of the up *Atlantic Coast Express* arrived from their far flung West Country termini. Geoffrey Freeman Allen visited here in 1952 to write the sixth article in *Trains Illustrated* magazine's 'Resorts for Railfans' feature - the fact that it came so early in the series being indicative of Exeter Central's standing as a centre of considerable railway interest. He described how, in preparation for the departure of the *ACE* its restaurant cars were hauled out on to the St David's bank by the station pilot. At 12.12pm the Plymouth and Padstow portions (having been joined together at Okehampton) arrived, drawing up ahead of the scissors crossing which sub-divided Platform 3 into two halves. The locomotive proceeding up the line to Exmouth Junction engine shed. The restaurant and Tavern cars would then be attached to the rear of the Plymouth and Padstow portions as one of Bulleid's powerful 'Merchant Navy' class locomotives backed down on to the front of the train. At 12.24pm the Ilfracombe and Torrington portions arrived, having been joined together at Barnstaple. The engine

The Avocet Line

One of the Great Scenic Railways of Devon & Cornwall

THE AVOCET LINE

wessextrains

Connecting People, Connecting Places

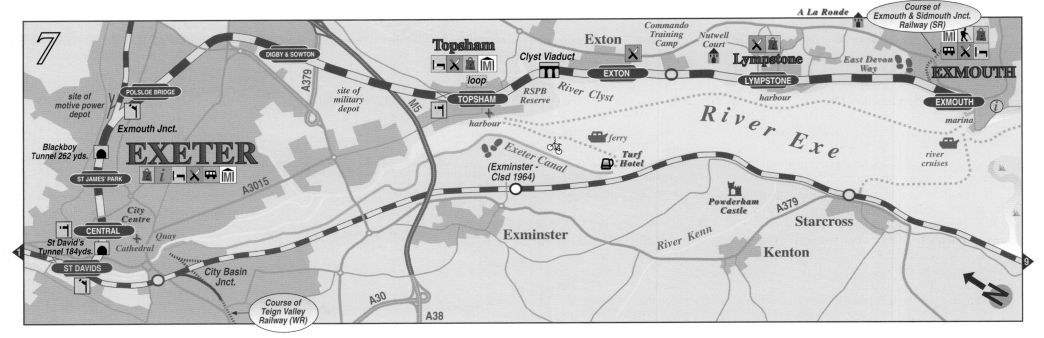

of this train departed to the shed via the scissors crossing, leaving the 'Merchant Navy' to propel the forward half of the train back on to the North Devon portion, thus completing the train's make-up prior to departure.

Shrubs thrive now where the through running lines once gleamed, and naturally there's no trace of the scissors crossing. Sometimes the Waterloo train is made up of two three-car Class 159 units, but it barely fills the 950 feet long platform, and such trains hardly reflect the dignity of those famous trains of the past. Forty years after the last *Atlantic Coast Express* took three hours to reach London, today's diesel units take roughly the same amount of time, but you are not offered the civilised comforts of luncheon or afternoon tea in the Dining Car on the way, whilst Bulleid's supremely comfortable coaching stock can only be enjoyed on the likes of the Bluebell Railway now.

Overlooked by Northenhay Gardens and Exeter Gaol, the Exmouth-bound diesel unit pulls out of Central station and passes through a cutting which leads to yet another saintly Exeter station - ST JAMES' PARK. Only roughly half the Exmouth trains call here, a quiet suburban halt shoe-horned between sloping allotments and the corrugated-iron

stands of Exeter City Football Club. Languishing now in the non-league Nationwide Conference, 'The Grecians' were founded in 1904, and purchased their ground at St James's Park for the princely sum of £40 from a local butcher. Some of their sturdier players down the years might have taken lessons from this benefactor, but in 1928 the club unearthed one Cliff Bastin who went on to become a star in the Thirties for both Arsenal and England. But perhaps the club's greatest claim to fame was that they provided the opposition for Brazil's first 'international' fixture in 1914. Heady days!

Blackboy Tunnel precedes Exmouth Junction, one time location of a massive motive power depot with an allocation in excess of a hundred locomotives. In British Railways Southern Region days it was coded 72A and contained a stellar allocation of 'Merchant Navy', 'West Country' and 'Battle of Britain' Pacifics. It closed in March 1967, looking after steam engines to the very end. A feature of Exmouth Junction was the Southern Railway's concrete manufacturing depot. It was established just before the First World War, and churned out all the structures from mileposts to footbridges which characterised the Southern's infrastructure for many years. The signal box was one of the first on British

Rail to be fully computerised.

The Exmouth train veers away from the main line, running over the rooftops of terraced streets which must once have provided homes for many a railway family, and reaching POSLOE BRIDGE station, a fine - if crumbling - example of Southern concrete architecture. High up on an embankment in a land of allotments, Posloe Bridge provides useful railway facilities for Exeter's north-eastern suburbs, and its single remaining platform seems well patronised, especially at peak hour.

Gradually the line curves away to the south, finding some difficulty in shaking off its hitherto urban environment. Business parks and industrial estates hedge you in as the train continues to DIGBY & SOWTON opened in 1995, not far from the location of an earlier halt called Clyst St Mary & Digby. Briefly there follows a rural interlude. There are good views to the east towards Woodbury Common topped by tumuli and an ancient hill fort. On the other side of the line a former American Naval depot falls into decay. The depot opened during the Second World War, the original siding being laid and opened for traffic in the remarkable space of two days - Network Rail take note! The establishment saw use until the Falklands War, latterly as a stores depot for the Navy.

Crossing the M5 motorway the line reaches TOPSHAM, the branch's only passing point. Although unstaffed these days, the station presents a pretty picture, with the station building and the signal box remaining intact, if not in railway use. With something approaching Swiss precision, *Avocet Line* trains sashay past each other under the remote but watchful eye of the signaller at Exmouth Junction. Old postcard views reveal that the station was originally built of red brick. It dates from 1860 and was the work of Sir William Tite, better known for more grandiose stations at Perth, Carlisle and Lancaster. Nowadays, it is a resource centre for the blind. At one time a branch curved round to Topsham Quay. It remained in use until 1957. Consignments of guano were transhipped from ships to railway wagons on the quay, and taken by train on a short journey to a fertilizer works on the banks of the River Clyst.

Topsham is approximately the halfway point on the line but you haven't even seen the estuary yet! Suddenly, however, a series of deep cuttings recede to reveal the Exe in all its not inconsiderable glory beyond low-lying marshland managed by the RSPB. Fox and deer are resident on the marsh, along with black-tailed godwit, redshank and curlew. A low-slung, metal viaduct carries the railway over the outlet of the River Clyst. Dense reed beds provide habitat for native species.

Houses with envy-provoking views herald EXTON, previously known as Woodbury Road. Its simple single platform is reminiscent of Glan Conwy on the Llandudno Junction to Blaenau Ffestiniog line. The station building is in domestic use. There was a siding here until the 1960s, and for many years a pair of camping coaches. Waiting now for the next train you can watch the tide's ebb and flow and processions of trains passing Powderham on the far side of the estuary.

Even at the height of their attempts to turn away custom in order to demonstrate lack of profitability, British Railways never resorted to meeting alighting passengers with an armed sentry. But that's the sight which greets you as the train pulls up at LYMPSTONE COMMANDO. This unnerving manifestation of the security-conscious age in which we live, is enforced by a notice insisting that 'Passengers who alight here must only have business with the camp'. You may quietly question the syntax, but you wouldn't dare discuss semantics with the gun-toting soldier behind the wire. The Royal Marines Commando Training Centre dates back to the Second World War, though the railway station wasn't opened until 1976. The lineside assault course looks as intimidating as the sentry's scowl.

Nutwell Court's neo-classical facade provides piquant contrast to the Commando Camp. Brian Watson suggested, in the first edition of the *Shell Guide to Devon*, that a Jane Austen character might step out at any moment. At one time it was the repository of Drake's Drum. Now it has become a well-known equestrian centre.

Remember how level with the water's edge you were at Exton? At LYMPSTONE VILLAGE the line is commensurate with the rooftops, strung about with a cat's cradle of electricity and telephone wires. The train has climbed through cuttings, momentarily out of sight of the riverbank, in order to negotiate a band of red breccia, a gravelly rock laid down by floods aeons ago, culminating in clifftops overlooking Lympstone's picturesque foreshore. In the early years of the 20th century buyers came down from London and the Midlands expressly to purchase Lympstone-landed fish. Despatch by the six o'clock train of an evening guaranteed delivery to Billingsgate early the following morning. Mackerel fishing was a speciality, over eighty vessels being registered here at one time. A hundred salmon might be netted on one tide. But factory fishing and pollution of the mussel beds in the Exe destroyed the bulk of Lympstone's trade.

Clickety-clack, clickety clack - the train runs down to Exmouth on its last lap, back beside the estuary's edge and often offering mirror images of itself across the Exe at Starcross. Only the regulars seem impervious to such beauty, from a visitor's point of view you want the journey to go on and on. Until 1967, EXMOUTH was the terminus of two lines, the other route having run down from Sidmouth Junction (on the main line between Exeter and Honiton) via Tipton St John's and Budleigh Salterton. It was from this direction that the through carriage detached from the *Atlantic Coast Express* would arrive. So did a Summer Saturday train from Cleethorpes, whose bizarre itinerary encompassed the likes of Lincoln, Nottingham, Leicester, Nuneaton, Birmingham, Bath and Templecombe. Operated by British Railways in the early Sixties, the journey took a boredom-inducing ten hours and forty minutes from the North Sea to the English Channel.

To cope with the traffic from both routes Exmouth station was a substantial four-platform terminus, given added presence by two imposing semaphore signal gantries (of four arms each) at its outer platform ends. A signal box and an engine shed and a goods yard created further sense of activity, and at one time there was even a branch line running through to Exmouth Docks. In the Philistine Seventies they demolished the imposing Queen Anne style station building to make way for road improvements. And yet, ironically, the traffic still often appears to run bumper to bumper. Offer up a grateful prayer for having had the sense to travel by train, and make your way to what's left of the docks for a crab sandwich.

Gazetteer

Exeter

See pages 14-15

Exmouth

Elegant, bracing and well known for its magnolias, breezy Exmouth combines the roles of residential dormitory for Exeter, seaside resort and gateway to East Devon.

Accommodation

THE BARN HOTEL - Foxholes. Tel: 01395 224411 www.barnhotel.co.uk Cosy 'arts & crafts' style two star hotel at far end of esplanade. Swimming pool and fine sea views.
MANOR HOTEL - The Beacon. Tel: 01395 272549 www.manorexmouth.co.uk Two star hotel where Franz Liszt once played the piano.
ROYAL BEACON HOTEL - The Beacon. Tel: 01395 264886 www.royalbeaconhotel.co.uk Three star hotel in which the King of Saxony stayed in 1844.

Eating & Drinking

EXMOUTH FISHERIES - The Esplanade (adjacent marina). Tel: 01395 272903. Delicious fresh crab sandwiches, jellied eels, shellfish etc to take away.
SEAFOOD RESTAURANT - Tower Street. Tel: 01395 269459. Dinners Tue-Sat.
BECKETTS - Tower Street. Tel: 01395 276734. Lively, enterprising pub/restaurant.
PAST TIMES - High Street. Tel: 01395 269306. Victorian tea rooms and restaurant.
THE GROVE - The Esplanade. Tel: 01395 272101. Pleasant pub with restaurant and garden on the sea front.

Shopping

Compact town centre offering all services within a couple of minutes walk of the station. Some old-fashioned, independent retailers (including the occupants of a thriving indoor market) catch the eye jaundiced by chain stores. Farmers Market on the second Wednesday in the month.

Things to Do

TOURIST INFORMATION - Alexander Terrace. Tel: 01395 222299 www.exmouthguide.co.uk
EXMOUTH MODEL RAILWAY - Seafront. Tel: 01395 278383. Impressive layout with lots of moving trains. Souvenir shop.
EXMOUTH MUSEUM - Sheppards Row. Open Apr-Oct, Mon-Sat 10.30am-12.30pm. Also Tue-Thur, 2.30pm-4.30. Local heritage displays in former stables and hayloft.
STARCROSS FERRY - runs Easter to October on the half-hour from Exmouth and on the hour from Starcross. Tel: 07974 772681.
STUART LINE -Tel: 01395 222144 www.stuartlinecruises.co.uk River cruises and sea trips including coastal excursions to Sidmouth.

Walking

South West Coast Path and East Devon Way. Enjoyable Blue Plaque Heritage Trail leaflet (available from the TIC) leads you to the former haunts of (amongst others) Lady Nelson and Lady Byron, two VC winners and a Royal mistress.

Connections

TAXIS - Abacus. Tel: 01395 222222.
BUSES - links along an East Devon coast sadly no longer served by rail. Service 157 runs hourly to Sidmouth via Budleigh Salterton. Tel: 01392 427711.

Exton

Comfortable, stylish pub called THE PUFFING BILLY (Tel: 01392 877888 www.thepuffingbilly.com) on Station Road within a couple of minutes walk from the railway.

Lympstone

Two pubs and a post office, a butcher/baker and a general store comprise Lympstone's modest facilities, but such statistics do scant justice to this former fishing village's considerable charm.

Accommodation

PETER'S TOWER - Landmark Trust . Tel: 01628 825920. Self-catering for two in a Victorian clock tower built in 1885.

Things to Do

A LA RONDE - Summer Lane (off A376 one and a half miles north of Exmouth station - bus service No. 57 will drop you near the door) Tel: 01395 265514. Pretty little sixteen sided folly built by two sisters at the end of the 18th century following their return from the Grand Tour. National Trust property with shop and tea room.

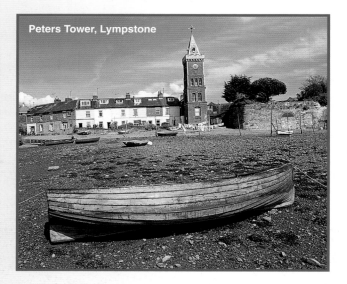
Peters Tower, Lympstone

Topsham

This romantic ghost of a port is, perhaps unexpectedly, one of the most appealing places to visit on any tour of the West Country's scenic railways. Topsham once had firm trading links with the Low Countries, a fact made evident in the architecture of its buildings. A number of houses are even built with Dutch bricks brought back as ballast in the holds of ships. Foot-sore from exploring, you can sit under the ramparts of the church and watch the comings and goings on the river. Perfect!

Accommodation, Eating & Drinking

GALLEY RESTAURANT WITH CABINS - Fore Street. Tel: 01392 876078 www.feeding-your-imagination.co.uk Award-winning restaurant with seafood slant plus accommodation with a nautical theme. Booking essential.
LA PETITE MAISON - Fore Street. Tel: 01392 873660 www.lapetitemaison.co.uk Outstanding French restaurant.
BROADWAY HOUSE - Fore Street. Tel: 01392 873465 www.broadwayhouse.com Ivy-clad, Georgian tea room also offering accommodation.
REKA DOM - The Strand. Tel: 01392 873385 www.rekadom.co.uk Comfortable accommodation in 17th century merchants house with impressive watchtower. Organic home cooking.
THE TURF - Turf Lock. Tel: 01392 833128 www.turfpub.net Incomparable, slate-hung old pub in splendidly isolated setting beside the entrance lock of the Ship Canal. Access from Topsham by ferry (see below). Exminster-brewed Ferryman bitter and Otter ales from Honiton. Wide choice of food plus bed & breakfast.

Shopping

The abundant presence of wine merchants, jewellers, dress shops, antiques, galleries, millineries and book shops, in addition to establishments purveying the more immediate needs of life, serve to underline Topsham's status as a honeypot. On the quay a former warehouse is home to three floors of antiques and collectibles - Tel: 01392 874006. Lloyds TSB bank with cash machine.

Things to Do

TOPSHAM MUSEUM - The Strand. Tel: 01392 873244. Open April to October on Mondays, Wednesdays, Saturdays and Sundays from 2-5pm. Local history made good plus Vivien Leigh memorabilia.
TOPSHAM-TURF FERRY - Tel: 07778 370582. Highly enjoyable ferry service from Topsham (Trout's boatyard) to Turf Lock at the entrance to the Exeter Ship Canal on the west bank of the Exe. The crossing takes approximately quarter of an hour. Timings vary according to season and tide - telephone to check. Special birdwatching cruises operate during the winter months, but you'll see plenty of interesting birds on the ferry in any case.
STUART LINE - Tel: 01395 222144 www.stuartlinecruises.co.uk River Exe cruises between Topsham and Exmouth, combined 'round robin' train/boat tickets available.

Walking

Short local walks to the RSPB reserve on Bowling Green Marshes. Cross on the ferry to The Turf and walk back to Exeter along the canal, or south to Starcross and the ferry back to Exmouth.

The Riviera Line

One of the Great Scenic Railways of Devon & Cornwall

THE RIVIERA LINE

wessextrains

Connecting People, Connecting Places

JUST imagine how differently rail travel might have developed if Isambard Kingdom Brunel's vision of the South Devon Railway had flourished - seven feet between the rails and powered by vacuum! The concept of an atmospheric railway was simple - or so it seemed to the dynamic Victorians - and if you are of an age to recall how, in some department stores, bills were 'blown' from counter to cashier using a pneumatic tube, some idea of the atmospheric principal might be grasped.

It may sound bizarre now, but the concept of atmospheric propulsion had been tried out previously on the Dublin & Kingstown Railway and London & Croydon West Railway, and when surveying the steep nature of the route between Newton Abbot and Plymouth, Brunel felt that the gradients involved would be beyond the capacity of steam. Instead of steam locomotives, therefore, trains would be propelled by vacuum, an iron pipe being laid between broad gauge rails through which a piston ran, sucking the train along the line as the air in the pipe was exhausted by a series of pumping engines located at intervals along the route. Sibilant and swift, at least for its time, the atmospheric railway operated for about a year until it was abandoned as unreliable in September 1848. Quite apart from anything else, you wonder how such a system could have survived, given the complexities of pointwork which were to characterise railway development. On a more mundane level, both the sea air and the local rat population were found to be having a detrimental effect on the leather flapping which kept the atmospheric piping airtight.

A modern power box oversees signalling in the Exeter district now. The former 'Exeter West' mechanical box has been preserved in working condition at the Railway Age visitor centre in Crewe. Barely a mile out from St David's you come to EXETER ST THOMAS, a listed station disappointingly shorn of its Brunelian trainshed in 1970. Nevertheless its frontage remains, an Italianate design dating from the doubling of the line in 1861. This section of line was built on an embankment and viaduct, not because of the lie of the land, but simply so as to avoid the need for level crossings on the even then busy south-western approaches to the city. St Thomas was never deemed important enough for expresses to call, but it was always, and remains, popular with the Exeter public in that it offered quicker access to the city centre than St David's.

There are some fine views of Exeter Cathedral to be enjoyed as your train seeks to escape from the city's urban clutches. Overlooked by gasholders, City Basin Junction marked the egress, eastwards, of a short goods branch to the Exeter Canal's terminal basin and, westwards, the commencement of the Teign Valley Line, a seventeen mile branch inland to Heathfield which linked there with the Moretonhampstead line until its closure in 1958, occasionally being used as a diversionary route when the coastal main line was being battered by storms.

Running parallel with the railway, the Exeter Ship Canal lays claim to being one of the oldest in the country, having been opened in 1566, a belated response to the construction of a weir across the River Exe in 1284 on the orders of the Countess of Devonshire, Isabella de Fortibus. Apparently she had been denied her customary tithe of the best of the autumn catch by the city's Mayor, so with a female sense of revenge undertook to block the river between Topsham and Exeter, thus bringing trade upstream

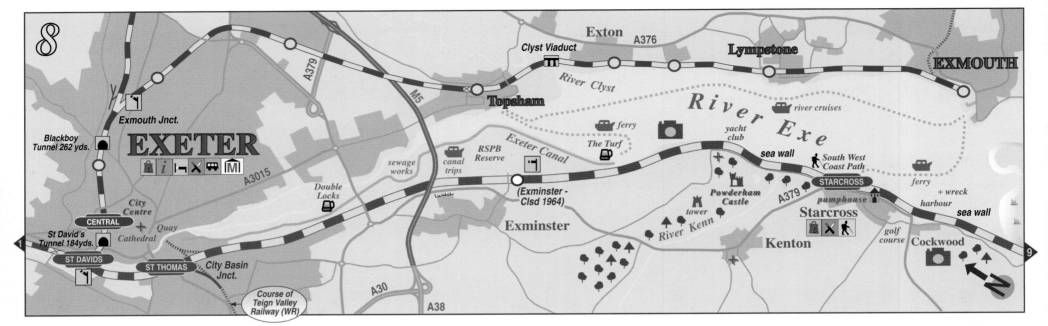

to a swift and, from her point of view, satisfying end. Three centuries later, the canal enabled Exeter to flourish once more as a port. Small sea-going vessels traded on it well into the 20th century. The last regular cargo was sewage, taken out to sea for disposal by a small coasting vessel until as recently as the 31st December 1998. Leisure craft still ply the canal, whilst its towpath makes for an entertaining traffic-free route for walkers and cyclists. A pair of moveable bridges might catch your eye - one lifts and one swings. The latter was built in 1936 by the Horseley Company of Tipton, a famous Black Country firm in canal bridge building circles. In 1944 it was subjected to mock attacks by Allied troops in preparation for the D-Day assault on Pegasus Bridge in Normandy.

The train reaches open countryside in the vicinity of Exminster. The station here closed during the Beeching era, though the station house remains in domestic use and the signal box has been adopted as a store by the Royal Society for the Protection of Birds who have a reserve on Exminster Marshes. There were 'water troughs' at Exminster in the days of steam.

Turf Lock, the entrance point to the Exeter Ship Canal,

is presided over by a remote inn called the Turf Hotel. Turner and Girtin stayed here when painting views of the estuary. A ferry runs to Topsham. The railway begins to run alongside the widening estuary of the River Exe. For some, the next two or three miles form merely an aperitif prior to the excitement of running alongside the sea. Others prefer the estuary's tidal changes and its rich bird-life, for which it is internationally acclaimed, providing a home for upwards of twenty thousand birds. Tourism has an irrational tendency to hibernate, but winter is a good time to take this train ride. Migrant birds from the Arctic and Northern Europe boost the local bird numbers.

Given the magnificence of the estuarial views, it is difficult to tear your eyes away from the waterside, but, inland, the scenery has its own rewards, notably Powderham Castle, the seat of the Earl of Devon, better known to train-spotters of a certain age as 'Castle' Class locomotive number 4080. Was it ever proudly underlined in your Ian Allan ABC? Knocked about a bit during the Civil War, its oldest surviving parts date, however, from the 14th century, but the bulk of it now is of 17th and 18th century origin. Located in a spacious deer park, there is a folly tower visible from the train on an

adjoining hillside, whilst the estate church of St Clement's stands in isolation alongside the railway; it was used by the Roundheads in 1645 as a base while they were attacking the castle's Royalist occupants.

The first stop out from Exeter these days is at STAR-CROSS where one of Brunel's atmospheric pumping engines remains more or less intact. Italianate in style, its campanile-like chimney is shorn of its loftier magnificence. The boiler house contained a pair of Boulton & Watt beam engines which derived their heat from three Cornish boilers. After the abandonment of the atmospheric railway, the engine house was converted into a nonconformist chapel and the boiler house was used by a coal merchant. In the recent past the building housed a museum devoted to the story of the atmospheric railway but is now a clubhouse for anglers and yachtsmen. Clutching an Exe Estuary Explorer ticket, you can alight here for the Exmouth ferry, as generations of Great Western Railway passengers were encouraged to do, an alternative to travelling over the deadly rival Southern Railway line. Long after Nationalisation was meant to bring cohesiveness to the railway network in 1948, the Western Region routed parcels for Exmouth via the ferry!

BEYOND Starcross (Map 8) the railway forms the sea wall - even through the sealed windows of modern rolling stock you can almost smell the ozone! The little harbour at Cockwood fills and empties with the tides and provides railway photographers with a photogenic foreground for passing trains. Look out for the wreck of the vessel *South Coast*. It broke its back on entering the estuary in rough seas in December 1943 and has lain there ever since. Soon the dunes of Dawlish Warren hove into view, a huge sand-spit jutting out into the mouth of the Exe which somehow contrives to satisfy a wide range of human inclinations, being variously a bird reserve, golf course and fun fair. None of these activities diminish its beauty.

Is there a more widely illustrated stretch of railway in the country, you ask yourself rhetorically, spellbound by the seascapes unfolding through the carriage window. The challenge, for photographers, is to discover fresh viewpoints away from the hackneyed scenes commonplace in the railway press. The South West Coast Path offers enough incentives. Take the trouble to walk between Dawlish Warren and Teignmouth and you won't be disappointed, at least if the light is kindly disposed towards you.

There are up and down loops, serving the platforms, at DAWLISH WARREN, which opened in 1905 when a rail motor service was introduced between St Thomas and Teignmouth. The old goods yard is occupied by a number of camping coaches operated by the Great Western Railway Staff Association. The down platform is protected from errant golf shots on the neighbouring links by a line of high netting.

With sea pinks flowering in abundance by the lineside, now begins perhaps the most classic seaside railway journey in the country, at least in England; champions of various lines in Wales and Scotland would doubtless be eager to argue the claims of their own favourites. Often there is shipping to be seen out in The Channel, and - in the absence of sea frets - fine views of the East Devon coast fading away towards Dorset.

On a warm summer's day, with the waves lapping serenely on the shore, it is all too easy to forget Brunel's daring in building the railway so close to the sea. In winter it's a different matter, when high spring tides batter the sea wall and waves lash, quite literally, over passing trains. On numerous occasions the line has been damaged. In the past

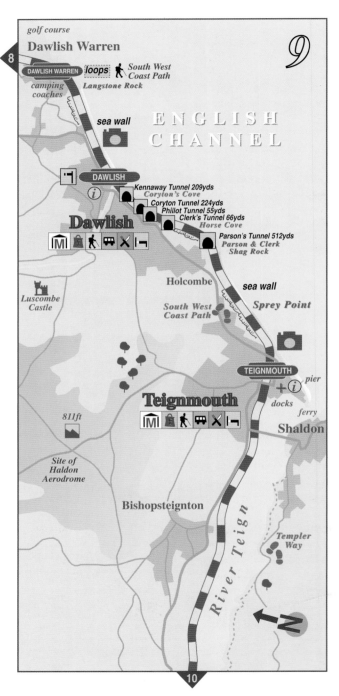

it was possible to divert trains inland by the Teign Valley branch or the Southern main line across the top of Dartmoor. In 1935, their coffers boosted by Government monies designed to blow industry out of the doldrums, the Great Western drew up plans to build an inland route direct between Dawlish Warren and Newton Abbot. A certain amount of initial work was undertaken before the Second World War intervened. Nowadays the only course of action when the structure of the line is threatened is to suspend services. Nor is it always strictly necessary for the infrastructure to be compromised - much was made recently of the inability of Virgin's 'Voyager' units to function when saltwater penetrated their air-conditioning systems. Not that stormy weather necessarily ruins the spectator's enjoyment of the sea wall and its passing trains. In *The Kingdom By The Sea* Paul Theroux wrote that 'the train on the rocky shore, rolling through the storm, was one of the most beautiful sights in the world'. Few modern items of rolling stock boast opening windows, but in the past on stormy days there was always the chance of being drenched if a wave hit the sea wall as you were passing!

Thanks to all the photographs that regularly appear in railway books and magazines, DAWLISH station looks familar, even if you have never passed this way before. Stopping trains slow to call at its twin platforms beneath a landward backdrop of oxide coloured cliffs topped by lines of Italianate villas. Along the promenade which tops the sea wall amorous couples spare barely a glance for the passing trains. Unless, that is, one of them happens to be a railway enthusiast, in which case any excitement aroused will not necessarily be solely of a sexual nature.

Brunel is said to have sketched the design for the original station building on the back of an envelope. Unfortunately it was burnt down in 1873. But the replacement is typical of Brunel, and quite probably unique in its proximity to the beach. Pulling away from the station, the train crosses a short viaduct before plunging in to a series of tunnels through the headland. When the South Devon line was doubled at the beginning of the 20th century the bores were enlarged without interruption to services. This extraordinary feat was achieved by inserting a continuous steel arch within the generous dimensions of the original broad gauge tunnels whilst excavating additional width.

There's a welcome glimpse of the sea again until a fifth

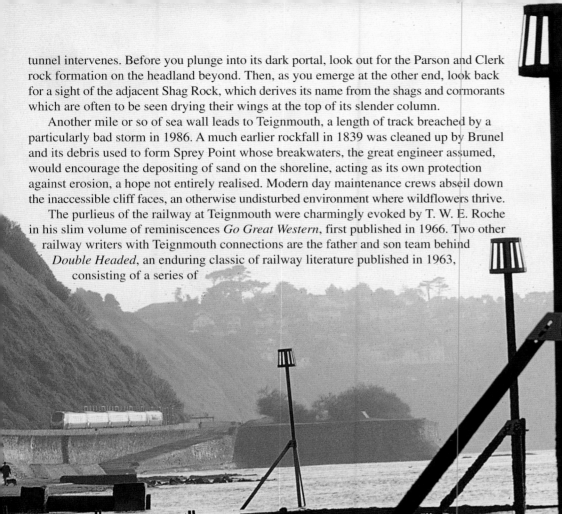

tunnel intervenes. Before you plunge into its dark portal, look out for the Parson and Clerk rock formation on the headland beyond. Then, as you emerge at the other end, look back for a sight of the adjacent Shag Rock, which derives its name from the shags and cormorants which are often to be seen drying their wings at the top of its slender column.

Another mile or so of sea wall leads to Teignmouth, a length of track breached by a particularly bad storm in 1986. A much earlier rockfall in 1839 was cleaned up by Brunel and its debris used to form Sprey Point whose breakwaters, the great engineer assumed, would encourage the depositing of sand on the shoreline, acting as its own protection against erosion, a hope not entirely realised. Modern day maintenance crews abseil down the inaccessible cliff faces, an otherwise undisturbed environment where wildflowers thrive.

The purlieus of the railway at Teignmouth were charmingly evoked by T. W. E. Roche in his slim volume of reminiscences *Go Great Western*, first published in 1966. Two other railway writers with Teignmouth connections are the father and son team behind *Double Headed*, an enduring classic of railway literature published in 1963, consisting of a series of

essays by Gilbert Thomas and his son David St John who went on to co-found the publishers David & Charles. Pacifist, poet and publisher, Gilbert Thomas also wrote *Paddington to Seagood*, the story of an O gauge model railway strictly operated (with Bassett-Lowke locomotives) to good old Great Western values.

Veering inland, the train comes to a halt at TEIGNMOUTH, a substantial stone-built station - one might almost say palatial - which dates from 1894, being executed in the jaunty French Pavilion style which typified the Great Western's *fin de siecle* approach to architecture. What hoardes it must have witnessed in its heyday. If anything, now, it seems cut off from the town by a busy road, but it retains its booking hall, and a cheerful refreshment room that harks back to the good old days of British Transport Catering in its approach and ambience. In the 1930s you had two means of arriving in Teignmouth under the auspices of the Great Western Railway - by train, or by aeroplane! Two flights a day in each direction were operated between Plymouth and Cardiff in six seater Westland Wessex aircraft, calling at Haldon Aerodrome in the hills above Teignmouth en route.

In the past there were goods facilities beyond the station and a line running down to the quay to facilitate the transhipment of ball clay. Teignmouth remains a busy port, with often up to half a dozen fairly sizeable ships jostling for space in its docks, timber, animal feeds and fertilizer coming in and clay going out. But the clay comes down from opencast workings north-east of Newton Abbott by lorry now; no longer rail, let alone by barge as was once the case. Teignmouth harbour bristles with all manner of vessels, not least the seine boats and gigs, once used by fishermen and pilots, but now adopted for a highly competitive form of rowing which has a stronghold in the neighbourhood.

Four miles in length and up to half a mile wide, the estuary of the Teign provides train travellers with a mirror image of the Exe, so that the whole journey between Exeter and Newton Abbot forms itself into a watery concerto. The Teign rises on Dartmoor, not far from Okehampton. The railway precludes public access to much of the estuary's northern shoreline, but the Templer Way follows the southern shore and makes for a fine walk between Teignmouth and Newton Abbot railway stations.

WITH the distinctive 'fang-like' rocks of Haytor visible to the north-west, the train slows for NEWTON ABBOT station, running between the town's National Hunt race-course and the residual sidings of Hackney Yard. This once important group of sidings was built at the beginning of the 20th century when the movement of freight by rail in the West Country was at its height. The yard was built out over the Teign marshes, which were stabilised with spoil brought by rail from Torquay, where a former tunnel had been opened out so that the line to Paignton might be doubled.

Passing under the A380 and curving sharply to the south, the main line crosses the reedy remains of the Stover Canal, promoted by James Templer to transport clay by barge to Teignmouth for transhipment into larger vessels. Opened in 1792, it was also used for the carriage of granite from Haytor, and even though eventually the railway captured much of its traffic, there was still a modicum of trade on it until the Second World War. Its barges must have presented a fine sight, rigged as they were like Viking ships with one huge sail. In later years strings of barges were towed by motor tugs along the canal and on down the estuary to Teignmouth.

Running in from the north west, but rusty these days, is the route of the Moretonhampstead branch line, closed to passenger services in 1959, notwithstanding its value for guests staying at the railway-owned Manor House Hotel, recently taken up by Peter de Savary and renamed the Bovey Castle. The track was retained for clay traffic which all seems to go by road now. A fine row of maltings - still in use - oversee your train's arrival at Newton Abbot station. Superficially, there is scarcely any evidence that this used to be a railway town, the South Devon equivalent of say Swindon or Crewe. Been and gone, in a hundred and fifty years, its locomotive works, wagon shops, running shed and marshalling yards. Why, even in the 1960s, it was home to a host of the Western Region's much vaunted diesel hydraulic designs, a stylish post-steam generation of motive power that had drawn its inspiration from German technology barely twenty years after Newton Abbot had been bombed by the *Luftwaffe*. If it was fitting that old enmities should evaporate so quickly in the spirit of commercial co-operation, it was correspondingly

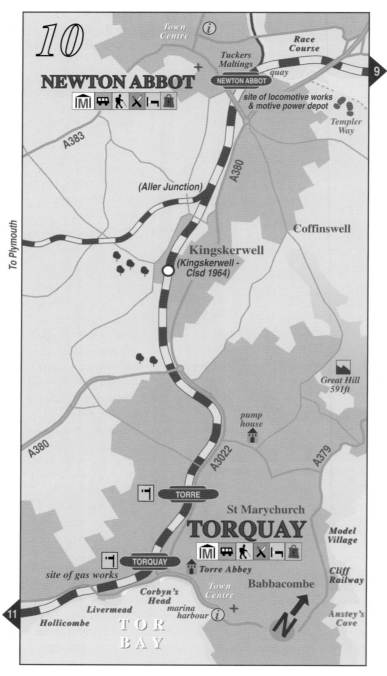

ludicrous that a fleet of over three hundred locomotives should have average life-spans of merely a dozen years.

Most of the station infrastructure dates from 1927. With its distinctive Mansard roof, the imposing main block has the look of Northern France or Belgium about it, in spite of being built of Somerset brick. It once contained the offices of the area locomotive superintendent, responsible for all motive power between Taunton and Penzance. He and his staff must have had their work cut out: engines were required in quantities for the branches to Kingswear, Ashburton, Kingsbridge, the Teign Valley and Moretonhampstead and for banking the heavy goods and express services over the notorious inclines between Newton Abbot and Plymouth. Virtually all the buildings of the motive power depot and works have vanished beneath the blandly ubiquitous premises of a business park. But a portion of the former works survives in use by a company manufacturing propellers, whilst the former wagon shops have for many years been used for warehousing by the publishing firm of David & Charles. Not visible from the train, the front entrance to their offices is overlooked by a handsome gantry of lower quadrant signals, rescued from the main line when re-signalling took place.

Before you leave Newton Abbot, compare the fabric of the buildings on the up and down platforms. The former attractive timber weatherboarding, the latter cement rendering. The explanation? On 20th August, 1940 two German bombers, accompanied by a fighter plane, attacked the station causing considerable damage and the loss of fourteen lives. The down side waiting rooms were subsequently rebuilt in the somewhat utilitarian form you see today. True to the prevailing spirit of censorship and propaganda, the following morning's *Western Morning News* played down the incident, drew a discreet veil over the casualties and quoted an eyewitness thus: "The way everyone behaved was simply wonderful".

The Torbay branch used to bifurcate from the main line at Aller Junction, a favoured haunt of railway photographers in days gone by. Here, on Summer Saturdays, a procession of trains heavily loaded with holidaymakers would be making their way to and from the resorts of Torquay and Paignton. Now the layout is simplified and most trains make their way to and from the branch back which would not have been sanctioned in the steam era in case of lineside fires, the railway passes beneath the Torquay by-pass. Locals will tell you that this is one of the most congested roads in the Kingdom. But then we all believe that of our local roads on this grid-locked island, and you can thank your lucky stars that you're on the train and immune to the frustration and anger which bedevils us all when we drive.

TORRE was the original terminus of the branch, the House of Lords at first barred its progress deeper into the enclaves of Torquay, an impenetrable redoubt of gentility. In time the vulgar railway was given authority to proceed, Paignton being reached in 1859. Torbay's morals apparently survived - to a certain extent - this being the era of Isaac Singer, sewing machine tycoon and prolific adulterer, buried in a mausoleum in Torquay in 1875, having fathered twenty-four children. His third son, Paris, inherited not only a good deal of his father's fabulous wealth, but his powerful libido too, counting among his mistresses, Isadora Duncan, the ill-fated dancer.

Deep within a land of stuccoed villas and private hotels, timber-built and apparently about to collapse at any moment in the slip-stream of the next *Torbay Express*, Torre station endears itself to finer railway sensibilities, appropriately finding use as the premises of a dealer in antiques and curios. Its Great Western running-in boards remain intact, as does its lofty signal box, preserved in aspic, albeit disused. The goods shed has found new use as light industrial premises. Here was Torquay's freight unloaded, too vulgar to be dealt with at the town itself. Alighting here between 1907 and 1934, you could avail yourself of a tram. For the first four years of its existence the Torquay system used electrical studs between the rails which proved prone to wear and poor contact, not to mention being the cause of death of many domestic animals apparently oblivious to the warning notices. Brunel built an engine house at Torre for his atmospheric railway, but this form of propulsion was never used on the Torbay Branch. The buildings, however, remain, housing a vegetable wholesaler.

At 1 in 55 the train drops down into TORQUAY and the self-styled English Riviera proper. Architecturally the station echoes Teignmouth, but on a grander scale. After all you are alighting in the footprints of Edward Elgar, Scott of the Antarctic, Agatha Christie and, presumably, John Henry Lee, who was found guilty of murder in 1885 and hung three times at Exeter gaol, surviving all attempts to execute him, and thereafter having his sentence commuted to life imprisonment. Again, as with Teignmouth, the station cafe survives - seemingly a feature of many West Country stations - and a ticket office and travel centre engender welcome gravitas. All these facilities are on the down side. The up platform has fared less well, its windows lugubriously boarded up. Even when the rent is peppercorn, it is not always easy to find occupants for station buildings, and yet such handsome buildings cry out for use, even when, as 'informed sources' relate, refurbishment would cost a cool half million. The signal box, at any rate, leads by example, having become home to a firm specialising in apartment rentals.

A brief climb of 1 in 57 takes the train out of Torquay. At the top of the bank stood Torquay Gasworks which received its coal by train from Kingswear, whence it had been brought by sea. Suddenly the sea becomes visible, tantalisingly framed by red cliffs and a line of beach huts, making you glad that you had the foresight to wear your swimming costume beneath your day clothes.

at Newton Abbot. Veering away from the main line the branch climbs steeply past the site of the closed station at Kingskerwell. Sections of jointed track have the train beating out a rhythm which would have been more familiar to earlier generations of holidaymakers, excitement rising like the railway at the thought of journey's end.

At about a hundred feet above sea level Kingskerwell (which has a picturesque 14th century church to the west of the railway) marks the summit of the line before it descends towards Tor Bay. For the most part in cuttings, or screened by small jungles of vegetation

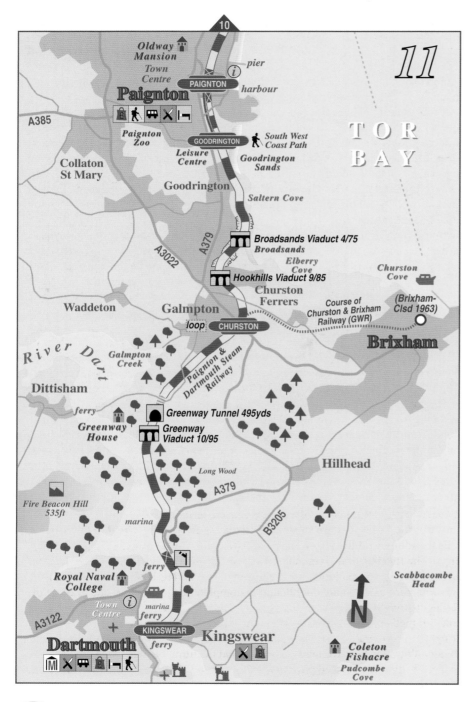

THE train glides down into PAIGNTON behind the backs of guest houses and hotels, with here and there a gap-toothed grin from the briny. Impatient motorists and acquiescent pedestrians observe your arrival, for the main thoroughfare between the town centre and the beach is obstructed by a busy level crossing. In the winter months this is the end of the line and, if you're reliant on public transport, to reach Dartmouth you will have to cross the road to the bus station. In the summer, however, you can make the journey more romantically aboard one of the trains operated by the Paignton & Dartmouth Steam Railway. Their station, right alongside Network Rail's, looks as if it has always been there, but it dates from their acquisition of the line from British Rail in 1972 and occupies the site of former carriage sidings. Though at pains to stress the commercial nature of their business - 95% of employees being full time staff - and its up to date methods of operation, the P&DSR take their cue from the traditions of the Great Western Railway. Chocolate & cream liveried rolling stock and GWR locomotive designs predominate. And even when you point out to them that the engine known as *Braveheart* is a British Railways Standard Class 4 design, they will reply with some glee that it was built at Swindon!

Private and public tracks make their way southwards out of Paignton in parallel as far as Goodrington, where there are sidings used for stabling the empty stock of those train operating companies which serve Paignton. During the British Railways era these sidings were enlarged and provided with a turntable to help cope with the sheer volume of holiday traffic experienced post war with the widespread introduction of holidays with pay. GOODRINGTON'S utilitarian station dates from this time. The P&DSR have plans to reinstate the loop here to provide increased flexibility on the single track section between Paignton and Churston, a reinstatement which will be especially beneficial when excursions are scheduled to operate over the line from further afield.

Goodrington and Kingswear lie virtually at sea level, but the railway which connects them climbs to a summit of two hundred feet at Churston. Of necessity, therefore, the steam engine at the head of your train labours hard as it pulls away from Goodrington, providing high drama for the sunbathers on Goodrington Sands. Correspondingly, passengers on the train are treated to wide views over Torbay; from the Thatcher Rock and Ore Stone islets off Torquay to Berry Head beyond Brixham. Given sufficient sunlight, suddenly you appreciate why this is called the English Riviera. Imagine yourself a young and impressionable locospotter back in the Fifties, torn between candyfloss, sand castles and a procession of steam-hauled trains: Kings, Castles, Counties, Halls, Granges, Manors, Moguls, Prairies and Panniers. It must have been tantamount to heaven holidaying on Goodrington Sands back then, and the sights and sounds and smells of the present day Paignton & Dartmouth Steam Railway go some way to recreating that lost era of innocence. Bless them.

On gradients of 1 in 71 and 1 in 60, made all the more demanding by sharply twisting curves, the line climbs towards Churston, rocky cuttings alternating with lofty viaducts. Once the junction for a two mile branch line to Brixham, CHURSTON is nowadays the home of the steam railway's workshops. It's a great shame that they couldn't have incorporated the Brixham branch in their operation, but this engaging little line, whose passenger services were push & pull operated (though often with the addition of a fish van or two) was closed in 1963 and a good deal of its trackbed has been built over. At the height of the season, trains are timetabled to pass at Churston. Hercule Poirot, and his faithful side-kick Captain Hastings, having travelled to Newton Abbot on the overnight sleeper from Paddington, arrived at Churston to investigate the murder of Sir Carmichael Clarke in Agatha Christie's *The ABC Murders*.

Now it's downhill all the way to Kingswear. Steam is shut off and the engine crew concentrate

on a cautious descent to the Dart. Greenway Tunnel swallows up the train, and when it emerges on the far side you sense a cathartic change in the scenery. Negotiating a lofty viaduct, the train offers magnificent views of the River Dart. Agatha Christie lived at Greenway House from the 1930s until her death in 1976. Perhaps she had an affinity with the Great Western Railway, for she is buried within sight of the main line at Cholsey, west of Reading.

In the good old days the *Torbay Express* would whisk you all the way from London Paddington to Kingswear; often King-hauled to the banks of the Dart, an auspicious means of reaching the English Riviera. Holidaymakers shared compartments with ratings bound for the Royal Naval College at Dartmouth. Completing the journey necessitated the use of a ferry, rendering that famous seafaring town a potential pitfall in any railway quiz, being the only station in the country without any track or platforms or trains, though in all other respects it had all the accoutrements of a typical seaside terminus.

With an authentic Great Western steam locomotive up front, it isn't hard to fantasise that you've made the journey all the way from Paddington still. Certainly the scenery remains spellbinding as the line hugs the riverbank for the rest of the ride down to KINGSWEAR. On the far bank Dartmouth's buildings are picturesquely heaped up against a wooded hillside, brooking no argument that you are duty bound to complete the journey by one or other of the three ferries at your disposal. Preservation has left Kingswear station remarkably unchanged and unspoilt. All that's really missing, as the train comes to a halt in the two-platformed, Brunel-roofed terminus, are the quayside sidings where coal was loaded out of the holds of ships on to railway wagons for Torquay Gasworks, and the turntable where the haughty likes of 'Castles' and 'King's' were turned prior to making their return journey to their more natural habitat on the main line.

Gazetteer

Churston
Map 11

Detrain here for the bus to Brixham, or walk to Galmpton Creek (which offers motor boats for hire on the Dart) or Greenway for the National Trust gardens and the ferry to Dittisham. Just outside the station, the Weary Ploughman (Tel: 01803 844702) offers food and accommodation.

Dartmouth
Map 11

One of the West Country's most attractive towns, Dartmouth is steeped in seafaring history. In the 12th century the Crusaders assembled here and, eight hundred years later, forces for the D-Day landings. Nowadays the only embarquees on a war-like footing are the tourists queuing for the ferries.

Accommodation
ROYAL CASTLE HOTEL - The Quay. Tel: 01803 835445 *www.royalcastle.co.uk* Very comfortable 3 star hotel in a prime position overlooking the harbour.
DART MARINA HOTEL - Sandquay Road. Tel: 01803 832580 *www.dartmarinahotel.com* Luxury 3 star hotel with views across the river and chain ferry to the steam railway.

Eating & Drinking
STATION RESTAURANT - South Embankment. Tel: 01803 832093. All day cafe/restaurant housed in former GWR 'station' building.
THE CHERUB - Higher Street. Tel: 01803 832571 *www.the-cherub.co.uk* The ancient home of a wool merchant which only became a pub and restaurant in the 1970s.
CAFE ALF RESCO - Lower Street. Tel: 01803 835880. Close to the lower ferry landing, open from 7am Wednesday to Sunday.
NEW ANGEL - South Embankment. Tel: 01803 839425. John *French Leave* Burton Race owns this unassuming restaurant which opens at eight in the morning for croissants and coffee.

Shopping
Charming shops proliferate in the delightful setting of Dartmouth's narrow streets. New and secondhand bookshops, several galleries and some excellent food shops. Markets on Tuesdays and Fridays.

Things to Do
TOURIST INFORMATION - Mayors Avenue. Tel: 01803 834224 *www.discoverdartmouth.com*
DARTMOUTH MUSEUM - The Butterwalk. Tel: 01803 832923. Local history displays with a maritime flavour.
DARTMOUTH CASTLE - Tel: 01803 833588. Waterside fortress dating from the 14th century under the care of English Heritage.
BRITANNIA - Royal Naval College. Guided tours available, for further details ask at TIC.
DARTMOUTH BOAT HIRE CENTRE - Tel: 01803 722367. Self drive boats for hire on the River Dart.

RIVER LINK - Tel: 01803 834488 *www.riverlink.co.uk* Coastal and river cruises many and varied. Offices on Lower Street.

Walking
South West Coast Path and Dart Valley Trail.

Connections
BUSES - First service 93 links Dartmouth with the South Hams resorts of Salcombe and Kingsbridge (continuing to Plymouth) whilst service 111 runs to and from Totnes. Tel: 0870 608 2 608.

Dawlish
Map 9

Made picturesque by Dawlish Water, which flows down through municipal gardens to meet the sea. Black swans and gaily coloured illuminations. References to Dawlish appear in *Nicholas Nickleby*. Up until the Second World War Dawlish was famous for the growing of violets, many of which were despatched by train to Covent Garden. Fine beaches, especially at Coryton Cove where you may share the waves with dolphins.

Eating & Drinking
SIGNALS - Station cafe at street level. Breakfasts, lunches and take-aways.
TILLY'S - Piermont Place. Tel: 01626 889999. Quaint cafe for light lunches and cream teas about three minutes walk from the station.

Things to Do
TOURIST INFORMATION - The Lawn. Tel: 01626 215665.
DAWLISH MUSEUM - Barton Terrace. Tel: 01626 865974. Open daily May - September. Interesting themed displays of local history including a small room devoted to the railway.

Walking
South West Coast Path.

Connections
TAXIS - Dawlish Taxis, Tel: 01626 888111.

Dawlish Warren
Map 9

All the fun of the fair: donuts, candyfloss, hotdogs and go-karts. Quieter spaces for bird-watchers out along the Warren itself. For details of accommodation in the Camping Coaches telephone 01626 888527.

Exeter
Map 8

See pages 14 and 15.

Goodrington Sands
Map 11

Beautifully maintained, award-winning beach backed by the Paignton & Dartmouth Steam Railway. Amusements, fast food, a family pub and a nice line in beach huts make this a perfect small resort. Ski West - Tel: 01803 663243 - offer pedalo and canoe hire, wet suit and water ski hire and speedboat rides. Quay West - Tel: 01803 555550 - is a modern waterpark with swimming pools and giant flumes. A small visitor centre devotes itself to the quieter pursuit of the bay's natural history.

Kingswear
Map 11

A shrinking violet in comparison to Dartmouth, Kingswear's houses are stacked, shelf-like in steep terraces above its highly picturesque riverside railway station and marina. It boasts three pubs, a small bistro, post office and general stores. KINGSWEAR CASTLE is available for holiday let via the Landmark Trust - Tel: 01628 825925. The National Trust's 'Arts & Crafts' period house at Coleton Fishacre (Tel: 01803 752446) is approximately 3 miles away on the South West Coast Path, or call Indicar Taxis on 01803 752626.

Newton Abbot
Map 10

Not as glowering as one would expect from a former railway town; stuccoed villas in leafy avenues apparently outnumbering the precipitous redbrick terraces which once belonged exclusively to the railway workers. Those in the know eschew the obvious but tawdry, take-away lined approach to the town centre along Queen Street, perambulating instead via Courtenay Park and Devon Square, encountering an enclave of Italianate villas built for businessmen when the railway came. Brunel worked on his South Devon Railway from premises in St Paul's Road.

Accommodation, Eating & Drinking
QUEENS HOTEL - Queen Street, opposite railway station. Tel: 01626 363133. Two star Best Western hotel with restaurant and bars open to non residents. Teignworthy ales on tap.
RAILWAY INN - Queen Street. Tel: 01626 354166. Friendly local alongside railway station. Bar food and Palmers (of Bridport) beers. Nice front covered terrace allows you to contemplate NA's fine station frontage.
Numerous take-aways of many persuasions on Queen Street within a minute or two's walk from the station.

Shopping
Farmers' Market every Tuesday, good fishmongers in Queen Street, and a nice old fashioned department store called AUSTINS both sides of the far end of Courtenay Street.

Things to Do
TOURIST INFORMATION - Courtenay Street. Tel: 01626 215667.
NEWTON MUSEUM - St Paul's Road, 5 minutes walk from the station. Tel: 01626 201121. Proof that you don't need to be big to be good. One room celebrating NA's unseverable links with the GWR. A collection of little treasures, including copies of William Dawson's watercolours of the Atmospheric Railway, audio recordings of local railwaymen's memories, and a 'working' signal frame. Ideal for a thoroughly entertaining hour between trains.
TUCKERS MALTINGS - Teign Road, 3 minutes walk from the station. Tel: 01626 334734 *www.tuckersmaltings.com* Traditional malthouse supplying many West Country breweries. Guided tours (including Teignworthy Brewery) Easter to end October, Mon-Sat plus Sundays in July & August. Specialist bottled beer shop on site.

Walking
TEMPLER WAY - 18 mile route linking Haytor with Teignmouth following sections of the Stover Canal and a granite tramway.

Connections
TAXIS - 1A Taxis, Tel: 01626 330011.

Paignton
Map 11

Proof that the English seaside resort can be simultaneously vulgar and invigorating, Paignton is Torquay's able lieutenant in the time-honoured provision of R&R.

Accommodation
PALACE HOTEL - Esplanade Road. Tel: 01803 555121. Three star hotel within easy reach of the station and overlooking the front offering, in their own words, 'affordable elegance'.

Eating & Drinking
ISAAC MERRITT - Torquay Road. Town centre, CAMRA recommended Wetherspoons open from 10am daily. Tel: 01803 556066.
LA SCALA - Queens Road. Tel: 01803 521832. Italian trattoria on seaward side of station.
OLDWAY TEAROOMS - Torquay Road. Tel: 01803 524263. Coffees, lunches and teas in Singer's former mansion.
It's a curious feature of Paignton that nearly all its fish & chip shops and restaurants are award-winning!

Shopping
Glance above the crass facia of the bulk of its shops and admire the latent Victorian and Edwardian dignity of its public buildings, many of them executed in a biscuity coloured brick unsullied by north country smoke. Gimcrack souvenirs east of the level crossing, more sustainable stuff to the west. ROSSITERS department store on Palace Avenue is splendidly old-fashioned. There's a model railway stockist and secondhand bookshop on Winner Street in the old town.

Things to Do
TOURIST INFORMATION - Esplanade Road. Tel: 0906 680 1268.
PAIGNTON ZOO - Long established zoo in 75 acres of grounds, many endangered species on view. Tel: 01803 697500 www.paigntonzoo.org.uk

Connections
TAXIS - Paignton Taxis, Tel: 01803 213213.
CAR HIRE - Chief Vehicle Rentals, adjacent railway station. Tel: 01803 663838.
BUSES - Stagecoach Devon's Bayline service No.12 links Paignton with Brixham from the bus station across the road from the railway station. Tel: 01803 664500.

Starcross
Map 8

Some charming architecture compromised by the busy road, all the more reason to come by rail.

Eating & Drinking
ATMOSPHERIC RAILWAY INN - across the road from the station. Tel: 01626 890335. Friendly roadside local offering lunches (sandwich to a steak) and railwayana.
Fish & chip shop to rear of (unstaffed) station building.

Things to Do
FERRY - runs Easter to October on the hour ex Starcross and on the half-hour ex Exmouth. Tel: 07974 772681.

POWDERHAM CASTLE - Tel: 01626 890243
www.powderham.co.uk

Walking
Exe Valley Way and South West Coast Path.

Teignmouth
Map 9

'Tinmouth' basks beneath its headland, reverberating with history and hedonism in almost equal measure. It is all too easy to rush through with the more aristocratic Torbay in your sights, but alight here and you'll come upon a refreshing little resort, given character by virtue of its working port and fishing colony. In its early 19th century heyday as a watering place Turner came to paint, Babbage - 'the father of the computer' - was married here, and Keats completed *Endymion* whilst lodging in the town. Not a bad roll call before the railway brought plurality in its wake. The town was an 'easy' target in the Second World War, no less than seventy-nine civilians being killed in air raids between July 1940 and May 1943. The firm red sand of the beach is exposed at low tide; simultaneously ideal for swimming and train-watching.

Accommodation
NESS HOUSE HOTEL - Shaldon. Tel: 01626 873480 www.nesshouse.co.uk Elegant Georgian hotel with colonial balconies in prominent position overlooking mouth of estuary. Excellent restaurant also.
POTTERS MOORING - Shaldon. Tel: 01626 873225 www.pottersmooring.co.uk Comfortable bed & breakfast overlooking the riverside.

Eating & Drinking
WHISTLE STOP - railway station. Customer-friendly station cafeteria. Cheap, cheerful and filling snacks and meals. Tel: 01626 777835.
COLOSSEUM - Regent Street. Tel: 01626 870000. Italian restaurant.
NAUTILUS - Brunswick St. Tel: 01626 776999. Seafood.
BLUE ANCHOR - Teign Street. Tel: 01626 772741. CAMRA recommended local down by the docks.

Shopping
The excellent QUAYSIDE BOOKSHOP on Northumberland Place stocks a wide range of transport material, both new and s/h. Tel: 01626 775436 www.milestonebooks.co.uk BRODEQUIN on Teign Street specialise in hand-crafted footwear - Tel: 01626 776341.
TRINITY MARINE on Hollands Road do a nice line in maritime artefacts and collectibles - Tel: 01626 778331.

Things to Do
TOURIST INFORMATION - The Den. Tel: 01626 215666.
MUSEUM - French Street, opposite the station. Tel: 01626 777041. Lovely little museum with several cabinets devoted to the town's rich railway history. Nice collection of Hornby Dublo model railway items. Material on Morgan Giles the yacht builder and Thomas Luny the marine artist together with much else besides.
FERRY - the Teign Ferry operates daily between Teignmouth and Shaldon from 8am. Tel: 01626 873060. Hugely recommended.

Walking
South West Coast Path and Templer Way (see Newton Abbot).

Connections
TAXIS - Alpha Taxis, Tel: 01626 773030.
BUSES - Stagecoach Devon service 85 runs hourly to/from Torquay via Shaldon and St Marychurch. Tel: 0870 608 2 608.

Torre
Map 10

Handy railhead for the northern and eastern suburbs of Torquay, but of little relevance to tourists. What shops and restaurants there are lie a 10 minute trudge to the south-east on a road bloated by traffic. For a taxi call Quick Cabs on 01803 297070.

Torquay
Map 10

Torbay's chief resort has the knack of re-inventing its magnetic charm for the benefit of successive generations. In this it is given every advantage by the brilliance of its setting which transcends the worst excesses of commercialisation. Comparisons with the Riviera are not entirely publicity driven. The climate does enable Torquay to soak up the sun and when it's really, really hot it *is* almost possible to believe you're in the south of France. The former harbour is now a chic marina, and throughout the summer months there are plenty of boat trips to be had across the bay. Torre Abbey Sands are within a couple of minutes walk of the station.

Accommodation
GRAND HOTEL - Sea Front and adjacent railway station. Well appointed and imposing Best Western 4 star hotel with Agatha Christie connections. Tel: 01803 296677. www.grandtorquay.co.uk
LIVERMEAD HOUSE - Sea Front. 3 star hotel half a mile south of the station but overlooking both the railway and the sea. Tel: 01803 294361. www.livermead.com

Eating & Drinking
PLATFORM ONE - station cafe offering snacks, grills and Sunday roasts.
NO.7 - Beacon Terrace. Bistro with the emphasis on seafood overlooking harbour. Tel: 01803 295055.
ORESTONE THE ELEPHANT - Beacon Terrace. Tel: 01803 200044. Stylish modern restaurant/bar open daily 11am-11pm.

Shopping
Copious and credit-sapping!

Things to Do
TOURIST INFORMATION - Vaughan Parade (the Harbour). Tel: 0906 680 1268.
TORRE ABBEY - The Kings Drive. Tel: 01803 293593 www.torre-abbey.org.uk Open daily Easter to end of October.
TORQUAY MUSEUM - Babbacombe Road. Tel: 01803 293975. Open daily Monday to Saturday, plus Sundays in high season. Local history and Agatha Christie.
WESTERN LADY - ferry service across the bay to Brixham. Tel: 01803 297292.

Connections
TAXIS - Torbay Taxis, Tel: 01803 558558.
CAR HIRE - Hertz, railway station. Tel: 01803 294786. Bay Buggy Hire - station forecourt, Tel: 01803 203333.

RAILWAY journeys are not solely about getting from A to B, often you are travelling through history as well. At the beginning of the 20th century most of the Tamar Valley's mines were worked out and a good deal of emigration was taking place. A one-way ticket to the USA from Gunnislake cost ten guineas. In April 1912 five unemployed Cornish miners joined the train at Gunnislake at the beginning of a journey that would take them to a new life in the New World. They changed at Bere Alston and at Salisbury with tickets made out to Southampton where they were to board a new ship called *Titanic*.

You might ponder on such matters of chance and fate as you make your way from Plymouth to Gunnislake on what is perhaps the West Country's most unlikely railway survival. The line continues to flourish largely because of the geography of the rivers Tamar and Tavy which precludes road improvements and ensures a steady demand by commuters and schoolchildren for the services that the line offers. There is an almost equally vibrant flow in leisure-seekers who have come to value the line's easy access to the beautiful landscapes of the Bere peninsula and Tamar river.

Rationalisation has reduced Plymouth's station count to one. Vanished the Great Western Railway's Millbay terminus; vanished the Southern's Friary, all services now being concentrated at the through station formerly known as North Road on the northern perimeter of the city centre. Remote enough to offer views from Platform 8 across a hillside of allotments to the floodlights of Plymouth Argyle's Home Park football stadium. Dominated by a 1960s skyscraper (once proudly - if indiscriminatingly - erected as the Headquarters of British Rail's Plymouth Traffic Division), often windswept, and apparently bereft of much character at all, there are corners of 'North Road' which repay closer inspection. The buildings on the far island platform bear handsome raised sans serif lettering dating from a rebuilding programme which commenced in 1938 only to be blown off course by the war. Above the canopies there are slate-hung offices and lift shafts. But in the context of the Tamar Valley Line, Plymouth is perhaps merely a preface, and you will be anxious, no doubt, to be making tracks in the general direction of more obviously scenic surroundings.

Not that the train escapes urban clutches without a struggle. Pulling out of the station, past Plymouth's 1960s power signal box, there are brief views to the south of the triangle of lines which once led to the Great Western terminus at Millbay; and their Ocean Terminal too, from which boat trains hastened privileged passengers up to London in a fierce (and ultimately tragic) rivalry with the London & South Western. Racing ended abruptly on the 1st July, 1906 when a South Western boat train came off the bend at Salisbury, killing twenty-four of its forty-three passengers. It comes as something of a surprise to learn that the boat trains continued running until as recently as 1971, though in latter years the passengers had been made up more of immigrants - particularly from the West Indies - than returning, well-heeled builders of the British Empire. Such contrasts in human fortune are reflected in the sombre housing zones which separate Plymouth from Devonport, and one's conscience is pricked to be setting off to explore the lovely Tamar Valley when less fortunate souls eke out an existence here.

Deep cuttings lead to DEVONPORT which boasted stations on both the Great Western and South Western routes out of Plymouth; the geographical oddity being that the former's trains were heading off into deepest Cornwall, whilst - running in apparently the same

The Tamar Valley Line

One of the Great Scenic Railways of Devon & Cornwall

TAMAR VALLEY LINE

wessextrains

Connecting People, Connecting Places

direction - the latter's were London bound. Nowadays the Tamar Valley train uses the old Great Western station, though originally - and, in fact, up until 1964 - it would have followed the London & South Western's separate route via Devonport, as depicted on the map.

Without getting bogged down in too much detail, it is interesting to learn that the London & South Western Railway's original Devonport station was a huge, barn-like terminus covered by an imposing overall roof enhanced by glazed endscreens. When the line was opened through from Tavistock in 1890, the station's west-facing end walls were pierced to create a through station. Regrettably, the station lost its roof to bomb damage during the Second World War and was demolished altogether to make way for a technical college after trains were diverted on to the Great Western's parallel route to St Budeaux.

Bit by bit, you see, we're beginning to piece together the fissured railway background from which the present day Tamar Valley Line is derived. Railway history rarely comes conveniently in one fell swoop! DOCKYARD and KEYHAM request stops follow in swift succession, weekday tea-time trains often filling as workers and schoolchildren make their way back to the Bere peninsula. For them the warships docked on the left-hand side of the train, glimpsed through turrets, towers and cranes and over rooftops, are as invisible as flock wallpaper. Visitors, on the other hand, will be fascinated by this reassuring evidence that we are still a naval power, and today's custodians of British dominion play football beneath the embankment with the same haughty insouciance that Drake displayed at bowls on The Hoe. Beyond Keyham station a line disappears into the docks. Not only do the workshops within undertake the maintenance of naval vessels, from time to time they turn their hands to railway rolling stock repair as well.

At ST BUDEAUX a connection laid in wartime reconnects us to Southern territory. St Budeaux Victoria Road is revealed as a pretty little station in old photographs, its now trackless down platform linked to a booking office at road level by a lengthy covered walkway. All gone: though in the undergrowth you might descry a yellow mile post informing those who care to know such things that they are currently 227 miles from Waterloo. All services

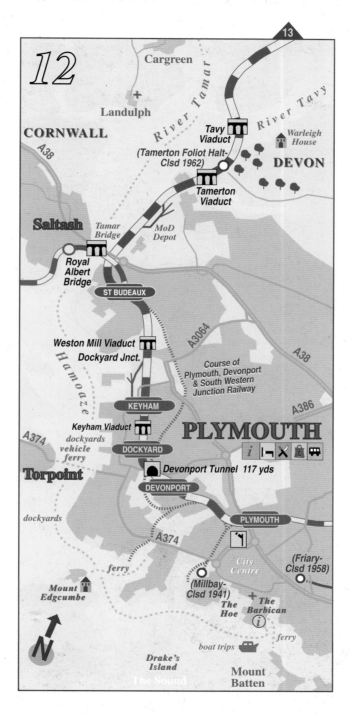

pause at St Budeaux so that the driver can access the branch's token from a cabinet on the platform, his authority to proceed up the branch in the reassuring knowledge that no other train can be on the line.

Gathering speed, the train burrows beneath the main line to Penzance and ricochets through sheer cuttings to almost river level before passing beneath the Tamar bridges; Brunel's tubular masterpiece of 1859 alongside its more utilitarian suspension neighbour, which brought an abrupt end to the Saltash road ferry upon its opening in 1961. Further down the Hamoaze the Torpoint Vehicle Ferry still plies for those romantics who like to think of Cornwall as a foreign country, the reaching of which deserves the symbolically baptismal element of a saltwater voyage. The train, for the moment, contents itself with journeying up the Devon bank of the Tamar estuary, offering interesting appraisals of naval barges moored against sundry jetties, a more sanguine view than the engimatically unsettling buildings of the armament depot on the landward side of the line, its bunkers linked to the railway but, judging by the rusty tracks, rarely used, which is probably, on reflection, a good sign.

TAMERTON FOLIOT sounds like a station that's escaped from a 1930's detective novel. In truth it escaped from reality in 1962, no longer consigning quantities of local strawberries and rabbits to Covent Garden and Smithfield respectively, as had been the habit in its heyday.

The yawning mouth of the River Tavy was bridged by the engineers of the Plymouth, Devonport & South Western Junction Railway between 1888 and 1890. It cost the then not inconsiderable sum of fifty thousand pounds. Its supporting pillars go down some eighty feet into the river's bed. Masonry arches support the approach from either side to eight bowstring girders a hundred and twenty feet long. Impressive as these statistics are, they do dry justice to the viaduct's beauty, best appreciated, not from the train of course, but from a passing Tamar river trip.

PD&SWJR? Well yes, perhaps we should have explained earlier that a nominally independent company built this line to provide the London & South Western with a clear run into Plymouth from Lydford in place of running rights over the Great Western's single track branch from Launceston and Tavistock.

CUTTINGS and embankments abound, the latter offering grandstand views. To the west you can see over the Tamar to Cargreen, from which a ferry was worked across to the Bere peninsula until the Second World War, enjoying a heyday in the transport of market gardening from the districts around Landulph and Botus Fleming to the station at Bere Ferrers. To the north-west Kit Hill is topped by its distinctive chimney. To the east you can see the Tavy narrowing upstream towards Tavistock and its Dartmoor source.

The old signal box on BERE FERRERS station proudly displays an earlier spelling of the village's name - Beer Ferris. It looks so appropriate in its setting that it comes as a surprise to learn that the cabin was formerly at Pinhoe, east of Exeter, being re-erected here by the enthusiastic owner of the *Tamar Belle*. This charming collection of railway relics includes a museum of local and railway history, a dining car, and a pair of Gresley teak carriages which can be rented out for holiday accommodation or bed & breakfast.

On the 24th September, 1917 a troop train bound for Salisbury with a contingent of New Zealand soldiers, recently landed at Plymouth, came to a halt at a signal in Bere Ferrers station. The soldiers had been told to expect a stop for food, and ten of them hungrily got down from their carriage towards the rear of the train. Perhaps it was the done thing to walk on the track 'down under', but they found themselves on the 'down' main line just as a Waterloo to Plymouth express rounded the curve. Nine were killed instantly, the tenth died on his way to hospital. It was a poignant way to meet death, on the other side of the world from their home. Not on the battlefields of Flanders as might have been their expected fate, but in a quiet Devon village.

In happier times Bere Ferrers was the location of Mr Jackson's Tea & Fruit Garden, attracting large crowds by train for strawberry cream teas. In 1928, 36,130 tickets were collected at the station. Other significant figures include the despatch of 2,963 milk churns, 49 wagons of livestock, and an income of 300 pennies for use of the lavatory. When war returned to the West Country, during the Plymouth Blitz, thousands of its citizens left the city at night to find shelter in the surrounding countryside. Extra carriages were added to the Tamar Valley trains, as villages on the line opened churches, schools and community halls for these 'refugees'

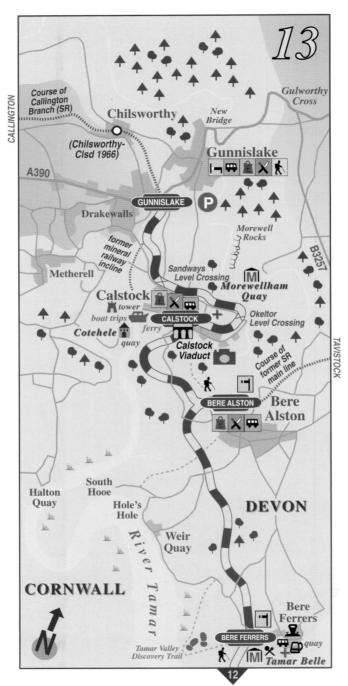

to sleep in.

Pulling away from Bere Ferrers, and still climbing at 1 in 73, the train sails across a high embankment. All that railwayana may have put you in mind of the past and this line's old expresses, the Plymouth portions of such once well-known and well-loved trains as the *Devon Belle* and the *Atlantic Coast Express*. What steam aficionados would give now for this diesel unit to suddenly transform itself into a train of green carriages behind a Bulleid Pacific or a Drummond T9: to stand in the corridor with the window down inhaling the soft scents of the peninsula's farmlands. A number of Bulleid's 'West Country' Pacifics bore names local to the area: *Calstock*, *Bere Alston*, *Callington* and *Tamar Valley*.

Cuttings envelop you. Some of them startlingly deep, as the line slices across the natural grain of the countryside. The Tamar plays hide and seek. Down on its Devon bank lie Weir Quay and Hole's Hole, former points of distribution for market garden produce which, before the railway was built, would be carried by market boat downstream to Plymouth. Fruit and vegetable growing, once such a key facet of the Tamar Valley's economy, has dwindled in the face of foreign imports and railway retrenchment. This is a shame, because the steep, sun-trapped slopes of the valley sides are particularly fecund. A moderate amount of market gardening remains. But now it seems necessary to augment the local climate with the erection of ugly poly-tunnels.

In essence the railways both gave birth to and brought about the death of a horticultural revolution on both banks of the Tamar. In 1862 a local grower, James Walter Lawry, on a visit to London was astonished to find that a pound of strawberries cost half a crown when they were just sixpence in Devonport. Sensing scope for undreamt of profit margins, Lawry and other Tamar Valley growers began expanding their businesses, felling trees to increase their acreage, drawing labour from the failing mining industry, and relying on the Great Western Railway initially (and subsequently the London & South Western Railway) to transport their produce, in ever increasing tonnages, up country.

For the best part of a century market gardening flourished in the Tamar Valley. At its zenith perhaps ten thousand people found varying degrees of employment in the trade. Not only strawberries, but gooseberries, cherries, rhubarb, and apples

also. Not only fruit, but flowers and vegetables too. Numerous varieties became associated with the district and bore romantic names such as 'Timperley Early' rhubarb, 'Tommy Friendship' strawberries, and 'Drooping Willow' cherries. The Tamar 'Double White' daffodils were despatched by train in cardboard cartons, bundles tied with raffia and wrapped, open-flowered, in blue tissue paper. Windfall apples went in open wagons to cider factories in Somerset, tubs filled with raspberries went to jam factories in Gloucester and Blackburn.

The Beeching Plan didn't only make life difficult for passengers. With the abandonment of the Southern main line across the top of Dartmoor, time-sensitive fruit, flowers and vegetables were no longer able to reach the wholesale markets early the following morning. At first British Rail magnanimously encouraged growers to bring their produce to Saltash or Plymouth, but later appeared to deliberately price themselves out of the market. No longer the country's 'common carrier', the railways couldn't be bothered being saddled with arguably unremunerative consignments. Effectively the railways had both enabled and annulled an entire industry in the space of a hundred years.

At South Hooe there was a silver mine. In the middle of the 19th century it employed over two hundred people, but production had ceased by the time the railway appeared on the scene. One last embankment permits a glimpse of the river running down towards Halton Quay, on the Cornish bank, where a chapel marks the spot at which the Irish sibling saints Intract and Dominica landed in the 7th century. The quay was another calling point for the market boats.

It must have been quietly entertaining, on any given clement day between the 2nd March 1908 and 5th November 1966 to saunter on BERE ALSTON'S 'up' island platform and watch the Callington branch train providing connections to and from the main line, or witness sporadic

shunting in the goods yard, or watch cartons of Tamar Valley flowers being loaded on to an evening train, so that they could be freshly displayed by the capital's florists the following morning. The London line still curves tantalisingly eastwards beyond the end of the former down platform, but it peters out within less than a hundred yards, six miles short of even Tavistock, which surely should have retained its railway service when the section west of Okehampton was severed back in 1968. What crass errors of judgement we perpetrated in the nineteen sixties and seventies. Lines so easily ripped up then, are not so easily relaid now. Several local initiatives have investigated re-opening the route between Bere Alston and Tavistock to take pressure off the A386, but since Privatisation the complexities and bureaucracies of railway reinstatement have become almost too difficult and expensive to contemplate.

Thus Bere Alston is no longer a junction in the true sense of the term; but, in the context of this extraordinary survival, it is the point at which the train reverses. Once that is, that the guard has used the key on the wooden train staff to unlock the point and throw the lever so that the blade will point the train in the direction of Calstock. While he's performing this ancient railway rite, spare a glance for the station fabric, still hauntingly and picturesquely - in a timeworn sort of way - redolent of its lost junction status: a disused signal box, two telegraph poles, a stone-built goods shed, an up side waiting room, and a down side station building that retains a hand-some valanced canopy and some vestiges of humanity in the continued domestic use of the station house. All combining to project a sum greater than its parts.

The formalities of reversal complete, the train departs along a stretch of line that was opened in 1908 to link the Cornish mining town of Callington with the Plymouth, Devonport & South Western Junction Railway's main line. The inhabitants of Callington, Gunnislake and Calstock had been campaigning to be linked to the railway network for some time. Hitherto the only railway in their neighbourhood was a 3ft 6ins gauge mineral line opened in 1872 to connect the mines with the quay at Calstock, from whence the coppers and tins and arsenics and ores were despatched to the outside world. To reach the riverside at Calstock, a 1 in 6 inclined plane was employed, using a counterbalance system to raise and lower wagons.

At first it was envisaged that the line would be built to 3ft 6ins gauge throughout, alleviating any need to convert the existing route between Callington and Calstock, but this short-sighted proposal was sensibly revoked in 1905, and the decision taken to convert the narrow gauge to standard gauge instead. To advise on such matters a consultant engineer was appointed, no less a personality than Colonel Holman Frederick Stephens, son of one of the Pre-Raphaelite circle, and a Svengali of light railways; impecunious and otherwise. It is on record that he supervised conversion of the six miles from Callington to the outskirts of Calstock, to meet the new extension from Bere Alston, over a weekend; an accomplishment which rather puts our present day line-possession culture into context.

But if the gauge change feat remains impressive, it is the line's major engineering structure that attracts the plaudits and the photographers to this day. There was no avoiding the need for a high level crossing of the Tamar at Calstock, and the viaduct which resulted took three and a half years to build. We shall encounter it in a few minutes, but in the meantime we are corkscrewing around the sharpest of railway bends, dropping down at 1 in 39 through primrose-clothed cuttings, which briefly recede to provide a glimpse of Cotehele House and quay on the Cornish bank of the river. Then, suddenly, it is as if the train has grown wings, and we move slowly out on to the viaduct, a hundred and twenty feet above the river, to make our way with welcome hesitancy across CALSTOCK VIADUCT, one of the Great Railway Bridges of Britain by any criteria you care to establish.

Any earlier, and in all probability Calstock Viaduct would have been built of Cornish granite. Instead, the relatively new medium of concrete was employed, an astonishing 11,148 blocks of the stuff, albeit treated with granite chippings that had a mellowing effect on what is usually considered a rather brutal medium. There are twelve arches and the structure is 333 yards long. Carrying only a single track, its narrowness and great height combine together to create a bridge of considerable beauty, at its best when, unruffled by breezes, the river's surface is calm enough to provide a mirror image.

It was arches 7, 8 and 9, whose piers are in the river, which, not surprisingly, created the greatest difficulties for the Liskeard-based contractor, John Lang. No.9 proved particularly problematic, as no rock could be found in the river bed to provide a firm foundation. Additionally, it bears remembering that the Tamar at the turn of the 20th century was still a busy water highway, Calstock Quay being often thronged with schooners and ketches, whilst the river was also enjoying a heyday in pleasure traffic catered for by paddle steamers which would sail serenely up from Plymouth, packed to the gills with sightseers. After the branch opened, the inclined plane fell into disuse and a steam-powered hoist was erected on the Cornish side of the viaduct to lower wagons down to the quay.

Those for whom vertigo is easily induced will be grateful to reach the haven of CALSTOCK station at the far, Cornish end of the viaduct. Colonel Stephens designed the original station building here, using corrugated iron in a style familiar on a number of his light railways. Ideally, it might have been retained, along with the platform's picket fencing, but the whole site was rationalised in 1968, and in its place the pleasant little pastiche of a traditional shelter doesn't jar.

Turning east, the train negotiates a horse-shoe curve to climb the hillside at gradients of 1 in 37 and 1 in 40. So elongated is this arc, a brisk walk up the road will put you in front of the train, especially given that the diesel unit has to pause at an ungated level crossing and blow its horn. A plaintive sound which goes echoing through the woods above the river like a call to prayer. Now running in a westerly direction, the train emerges from a cutting at the foot of the graveyard of Calstock's 13th century parish church. Peter Denny, creator of *Buckingham Great Central*, one of the most revered model railways of all time, was once curate here. Pausing for another level crossing, you now find yourself heading north, and there are splendid views to the right past Morwell's towering rocks which lend the Tamar the look of Rhineland. Old chimneys hint that the landscape hereabouts must have looked remarkably different when mining was at its zenith, and it's difficult now to equate the peaceful scenery of the present day with all that lost activity.

Heaving a phlegmatic sigh, our diesel unit comes to a halt at GUNNISLAKE, the foreshortened end of the line. Five hundred feet we've climbed to get to this remote outpost of the railway network. Until 1966 the line continued around the top end of Kit Hill to Callington, or rather Kelly Bray, a mile to the north. A good enough reason by then to abandon the last five miles of the line in the face of mining subsidence and competition from buses which actually took you to the doorstep of where you wanted to go. But since then we have grown to appreciate what benefits a rural railway can bring: an environmentally sustainable, cohesive and robust mode of transport difficult not to love for its own sake.

Gazetteer

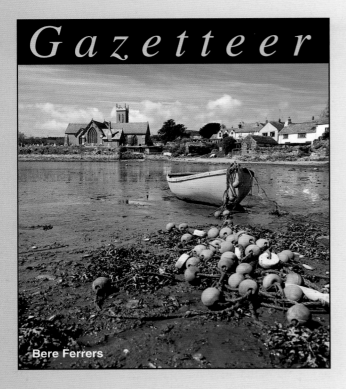
Bere Ferrers

Bere Alston
Map 13

Bere is thought to be a Celtic word meaning spit of land or peninsula. Certainly, without their railway, Bere Alston and Bere Ferrers would seem even further beyond the back of beyond. The village is a healthy tramp from the station, a state of affairs not uncommon in the West Country. Soporific now, Bere Alston was at its commercial zenith with the 19th century boom in lead and silver mining, and parts of the village still wear the demeanour of an up-country pit town.

Eating & Drinking
THE EDGCUMBE - Fore Street. Village local where the emphasis is on liquid refreshment as opposed to solid. Tel: 01822 840252. *Fish & chip shop and takeaway in village centre.*

Shopping
Co-op with cash machine, Spar, post office, pharmacy, butcher and sprawling secondhand bookshop - Tel: 01822 841638.

Walking
Tamar Valley Discovery Trail plus Village Trail leaflets available locally.

Connections
BUSES - First service 185 links the railway station with Tavistock. Tel: 01752 402060.

Bere Ferrers
Map 13

A smaller, sleepier version of Bere Alston with the additional delight of a quayside on the River Tavy. The war memorial, in addition to the local dead, commemorates the ten New Zealanders who died in such tragic circumstances at the railway station. In the churchyard, a common grave marks the resting place of cholera victims in 1849.

Accommodation, Eating & Drinking
TAMAR BELLE - Tel: 01822 840044. Two former Gresley teak carriages available for comfortable self-catering or overnight accommodation, but please give notice. Meals also available in an adjoining BR MK1 dining car. *www.tamarbelle.co.uk*
OLDE PLOUGH INN - village centre. Tel: 01822 840353. Charming 16th century inn: flagstones, beams, and archive views of the district, sun-trap patio at the back, various West Country ales and an excellent menu combine to make this a perfect pub - though *no* food on Monday evenings out of season.

Shopping
Post Office and village store about 5 minutes walk from the station near the quay.

Things to Do
TAMAR BELLE HERITAGE CENTRE - Tel: 01822 840044. Charming displays of local and railway history housed in a ex LMS Stanier sleeping car. 'Pinhoe' signal box is also open on an occasional basis for guided tours. *www.tamarbelle.co.uk*

Walking
Tamar Valley Discovery Trail - 30 mile walking route connecting Plymouth with Launceston. Village Trail leaflet also available locally.

Calstock
Map 13

In his never bettered *Shell Guide to Cornwall*, John Betjeman perceptively likens Calstock to a Cornish fishing village with a river at its quayside in place of the sea. Arrive or depart by boat and this illusion appears even stronger.

Accommodation
DANESCOMBE MINE - former arsenic mine engine house refurbished by the Landmark Trust for holiday lets - Tel: 01628 825925.
NATIONAL TRUST HOLIDAY COTTAGES - holiday lets in properties on the Cotehele estate - Tel: 01579 351346.

Eating & Drinking
TAMAR INN - The Quay. Tel: 01822 832487. Very popular riverside pub offering a wide range of ales and food.
RIVERSIDE RESTAURANT - The Quay. Tel: 01822 832302.

Shopping
LEVINES general store.

Things to Do
COTEHELE - National Trust property accessible on foot from Calstock station, via ferry when operating - see below, or by Corlink minibus for which at least an hour's forward notice is required - see right. Fortified Tudor house set in acres of woodland with formal gardens. Working watermill, quay beside the Tamar with restored barge *Shamrock*. Tearooms, restaurant and shop - Tel: 01579 351346.
TAMAR PASSENGER FERRY - seasonal pedestrian links with the Devon bank of the Tamar (and walks to Bere Alston etc) and Cotehele Quay. Tel: 01822 833331.
PLYMOUTH BOAT CRUISES - Tamar river boat trips to/from Plymouth - Tel: 01752 822797.

Connections
BUSES - First service 79 connects Calstock Quay with Tavistock and Callington Monday to Saturday. Tel: 01752 402060.
CORLINK - flexible minibus service - Tel: 0845 850 5556.

Gunnislake
Map 13

Straggling, elongated village on a steep hill leading down to the medieval bridge which carries the A390 into Devon. This 'New Bridge', dating from the 16th century, was the lowest bridge across the River Tamar until the suspension bridge at Saltash opened in 1961.

Accommodation, Eating & Drinking
THE CORNISH INN - village centre 10 minutes downhill from station. Tel: 01822 834040. Food and accommodation.

Shopping
MACE stores, Post Office and the excellent TAMAR VALLEY BUTCHERS, Tel: 01822 832524.

Things to Do
MORWELLHAM QUAY - Tel: 01822 832766 *www.morewellham-quay.co.uk* Marvellously recreated Victorian industrial village, port and mine accessed by road via Gunnislake or via occasional boat trips from Calstock.

Connections
BUSES - First service 79 connects with Tavistock and Callington, Monday to Saturday. Tel: 01752 402060.
CORLINK - flexible minibus service - Tel: 0845 850 5556.

Plymouth
Map 12

Thriving modern city which bravely rebuilt itself after being devastated by bombing during World War II.

Accommodation
INVICTA HOTEL - Osborne Place. Tel: 01752 664997 *www.invictahotel.co.uk* Comfortable 2 star hotel near The Hoe.

Eating & Drinking
TANNERS RESTAURANT - Finewell Street. Tel: 01752 25201. *www.tannersrestaurant.com* TV brothers' restaurant by St Andrews.

Shopping
'High Street' shopping in the rebuilt sections of the city off Armada Way, curios and collectibles in the Barbican.

Things to Do
TOURIST INFORMATION - Tel: 01752 266030.
TINSIDE LIDO - Tel: 0870 300 0042. Magnificent Art Deco saltwater swimming pool beneath the Hoe.
PLYMOUTH DOME - Tel: 01752 603300. Award-winning interpretations of Plymouth's vibrant history. Inlcudes Smeaton's Tower.
NATIONAL MARINE AQUARIUM - Tel: 01752 220084.

Connections
TAXIS - Plymouth Taxis, Tel: 01752 606060.

The Looe Valley Line

One of the Great Scenic Railways of Devon & Cornwall

THE LOOE VALLEY LINE

wessextrains

Connecting People, Connecting Places

IF the proprietors of the Liskeard & Looe Union Canal hadn't seen fit, two-thirds of the way through the 19th century, to convert their canal into a railway. *If* that selfsame railway hadn't survived periods of impecuniosity to become absorbed into the Great Western Railway in 1923. *If* that famous and much-esteemed railway's plans in 1935 to build a new direct route between Plymouth and Looe, operated by speedy diesel railcars, had been realised. And *if* the Liskeard to Looe branch line hadn't escaped Beeching's axe by the skin of its teeth in 1966, then we would not still have this hugely quaint and unusual railway to enjoy today. Just how quaint, you will soon see for yourselves, and unusual? Well, for a start, travellers new to Liskeard, and intent on reaching Looe by rail, are surprised to find their connecting train lurking at its own quite separate platform at right angles to the main station. Furthermore, those with a well-honed sense of direction might be ever so slightly disconcerted to discover that the train they are about to catch to the south coast of East Cornwall facing somewhat disorientatingly north! Relax, this is all part and parcel of the Looe Valley Line's considerable charm.

When this guide was being complied work was taking place to refurbish LISKEARD station, including the exciting provision of a Visitor Centre and shop on the Looe platform. Patronside this, then clamber aboard your diesel unit, try and get a seat on the platform side, face the back, and settle down to enjoy one of the Great *Little* Railway Journeys of the World. All one's geographic uncertainties unravel as the train departs, making its way gingerly down a steep horseshoe curve, passing beneath the main line to reach the valley floor, some one hundred and fifty feet below. In 1906 six fortuitously empty carriages ran away down this 1 in 40 gradient, and but for the presence of mind of the signalman at the foot of the bank, together with the fact that a team of carpenters working in the sidings at Moorswater had knocked off early, a greater tragedy than the spectacular implosion of three timber carriages might have occurred.

This unusual overture to your journey along the Looe Valley dates from 1901, prior to that passengers were left to their own devices to make their way phlegmatically up and down the steep lanes between Liskeard and a station in the valley called, appropriately enough, Coombe. COOMBE remains open to this day, albeit served by only a couple of trains in each direction, and the track in fact continues northwards again, passing once more beneath the main line as it is carried across the valley on Moorswater Viaduct to reach a cement depot which receives regular deliveries by train. In the past this formed part of the Liskeard & Caradon Railway, completed in 1846 to bring copper and granite down from the moors above Liskeard. Coombe station has a quiet charm of its own, being overlooked by a former tweed mill, and from its lonely platform you can watch trains on the main line crossing the high arches of Moorswater Viaduct, noting, in that naturally observant way of yours, the remaining, ivy-clad piers of the original timber viaduct standing proud alongside their replacement of 1881.

The trains which don't serve Coombe reverse at Coombe Junction. In steam days, of course, the locomotive had to run round its train. Nowadays the manoeuvre is simplified, being reminiscent of the arrangement at Bere Alston on the Tamar Valley Line, and involves the driver changing ends and the guard descending from the train to operate the points. Once this has been achieved, the journey proper can commence, an enchanting

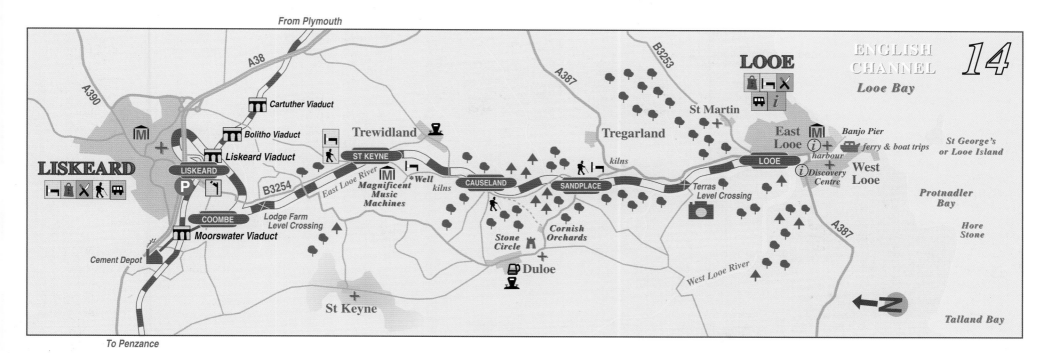

six mile ride down the bosky valley of the East Looe River oddly reminiscent of BB's children's book *The Forest of Bowland Light Railway*, a railway run, for those unfamiliar with this charming story, by gnomes!

It may be merely half a dozen miles from Coombe Junction to Looe, but with a maximum speed limit of forty miles an hour, and several sections where the train must proceed judiciously at just twenty-five, the ride takes around twenty minutes and you find yourself anxious to make every moment last.

ST KEYNE is the first of three wayside stations between Coombe and Looe. Its single bare platform is enhanced by a recently built shelter traditionally styled with a valanced wooden awning. Alighting here should be mandatory one feels, for a former watermill alongside the station houses a fascinating collection of music machines, whilst nearby, up a typically deep Cornish lane, burnished by primroses in springtime, is the ancient well of St Keyne whose waters are reputed to give mastery in marriage. What more incentive does one need!

Weaving its way along the valley between precipitous

grassy ridges glimpsed through a curtain of trees, the railway accompanies the cascading river, with here and there, to the experienced eye, tell-tale evidence of the former canal such as bridge arches and the timber stumps of lock gear. The canal first thrust its way up the valley in 1828, initially to transport fertilizers such as lime and sand inland to combat Cornwall's acid soils. There were twenty-five locks in its six mile course from Terras Pill to Moorswater. At Terras there was a lock-keeper responsible for the collection of tolls but all the other locks were operated by the boatmen themselves. Ostensibly the barges in use were supposed to be capable of handling a payload of twenty tons, though records suggest that in practice somewhat less was practical, for the canal was cheaply built and maintained and its navigable depths not all they should be: the locks above Terras were fifty-seven feet in length by thirteen and a half feet wide. Amongst the recorded cargoes were limestone and coal, sand and manure, ores, metals and agricultural produce. Following a number of successful years, traffic began to fall, to the concern of the company and its shareholders. Hitherto trade had been predominently uphill in character with little in return. The

canal company was grateful, therefore, for the discovery in the late 1830s of substantial copper deposits in the vicinity of Caradon Hill above Liskeard and, after the construction of a tramway to the canal head at Moorswater, trade was significantly boosted by the carriage of copper, and later granite from Cheesewring, down to the harbour at Looe. Indeed, these new traffics developed to such an embarrassingly high degree that the canal was unable to cope and the company chose to convert the bulk of it into a railway.

One can only cogitate on such a colourful history as the railcar winds down the valley through woodland which positively reeks of wild garlic throughout the summer. Some sections of the track remain jointed, and you are lulled by the muffled rhythm of the wheels hitting the gaps between the short lengths of rail.

CAUSELAND is the most hidden and unworldly of the intermediate halts. At one time it enjoyed rather spurious national acclaim as the smallest station in the kingdom. At this point the river lies to the east of the railway, beyond which the land rises steeply to a green-shouldered hill covered with yellow gorse in season. On leaving Causeland, the line

runs past Badham Farm and a development of self-catering cottages which might appeal as a possible holiday destination for the railway-minded.

Conversion to a railway was completed by 1860, and as far as the Board of Trade were concerned, the line was registered solely for the carriage of goods. Passengers, however, were discreetly encouraged, and although they couldn't legally be sold tickets, income was derived by issuing them with passes if they paid for the conveyance of their personal belongings, such as coats or hats or packages or umbrellas! In the face of Caradon's copper output declining towards the end of the 19th century, the still independent railway company eventually reinvented itself as a passenger-carrying concern. Considerable work was required to achieve the necessary standards: new track, signals, mileposts and, not least, the formal provision of stations. A good deal of capital was spent on these improvements without realising sufficient returns in revenue and the turn of the century saw the railway in a parlous state. What was needed was a connection with the main line at Liskeard. Several ideas were put forward, perhaps the most interesting being for a rack railway between Moorswater and Liskeard with a daunting gradient of 1 in 7! An even more radical suggestion was the construction of a line from Menheniot, on the main line east of Liskeard, to Looe direct, a scheme echoed by the Great Western Railway's proposals of the Thirties.

The link brought fresh impetus to the railway, a new traffic manager called Horace Holbrook was recruited from the Great Eastern Railway, and the formal opening took place on 15th May, 1901. Four hundred people travelled down from Liskeard to Looe on the first day with almost as many travelling in reverse. Unfortunately the last up train of the day ran out of steam on the steep bank between Coombe Junction and Liskeard, causing a large party of visitors from Plymouth to miss the last connection home on the main line. With true Victorian pluck, Horace Holbrook came to the rescue and paid for a special to take them happily home to bed. Obviously a man of initiative and drive. In due course he rose to become Assistant Station Master at Paddington.

Between Causeland and Sandplace the river exchanges sides with the railway for the remainder of the journey. A smattering of domestic properties border the line, notably, on the eastern side of the track, a thatched house with a private swimming pool in the prominent view of envious passengers. SANDPLACE station is located on a sharp curve. Here, in common with St Keyne, an attractive shelter of traditional appearance, built from brick and wood and steel, has been provided. When the rest of the canal was abandoned, it remained in use as far as Sandplace until 1901. Below the station at one time a loop provided siding space for goods being taken to and from a local estate. The Liskeard & Looe Railway remained nominally independent until 1923, although the Great Western Railway had been to all intents and purposes operating the line from 1909 onwards.

After Sandplace the woods recede and the now tidal Looe river widens in an increasingly beguiling manner so as to provide passengers - particularly those seated on the right hand side of the train - with gorgeous views irrespective of the state of the tide. When it's high the water laps almost to the edge of the track - when it's low wide expanses of mud are revealed and wildfowl and wading birds make the most of the opportunity to feed - look out for the white egrets with a tassel at the back of their heads. It's along this scenic stretch of line that many of the best photographs of the Liskeard-Looe branch have been taken over the years. Arguably the most nostalgic depict scenes from the 1950s with Churchward's elegant Prairie tanks in charge of a 'B-set' pair of non-corridor carriages in British Railways early red and cream livery.

Wheels screeching - or is it the seagulls - the train slows cautiously to negotiate the ungated level-crossing at Terras. The hooting of the railcar's horn in warning seeming to echo over the mudflats upon which long-abandoned boats slowly disintegrate. Offering widening views reminiscent - if proportionately less spectacular - of the railway's final approach to Kyle of Lochalsh, the Looe Valley train rumbles over its last mile of track to a truncated terminus on the water's edge a few hundred yards upstream of the ancient bridge that links the twin townships of East and West Looe. The Ticket Office is a recent improvement. In the old days the track continued to a fan of sidings on the quayside where transhipment was made to and from coasting vessels, but the route down to the bridge has disappeared under new developments: a garage, a health centre and a police station. Under a more rationally minded transport policy, this would have been an ideal opportunity to extend the passenger-carrying part of the railway on to the quayside itself, now a car park instead. Imagine what fun it would be to alight alongside Looe's fishing fleet amidst the aroma of freshly caught pilchards. Ah well, at least we still have the *Looe Valley Line* more or less intact, and the future bodes well, because the line has been identified as a potential pilot for microfranchising, enabling it to function in a semi or fully autonomous environment, a true Community Railway with local management able to project the railway and its services in educated response to the perceived requirements of locals and visitors alike. Full circle, then, to the line's 19th century origins, and the search will soon be on for a Traffic Manager as enterprising as Horace Holbrook.

Gazetteer

Banjo Pier, Looe

Causeland

Causeland's lonely platform offers access to the village of Duloe, a steep country mile to the west. Duloe is chiefly noted for its stone circle and 13th century church.

Accommodation
BADHAM FARM HOLIDAY COTTAGES - adjacent Causeland station. Tel: 01579 343572. Six 3 star rated cottages offering various activities and a grandstand view of trains on the Looe line.

Eating & Drinking
YE OLDE PLOUGH - Duloe village centre. Tel: 01503 262050. Slate-floored country pub serving Sharps Doom Bar, steak on hot stones and locally produced cider.

Shopping
Village stores in Duloe owned and operated by the charmingly named Katy O'Keefe & Father!

Places to Visit
CORNISH ORCHARDS - Westnorth Manor Farm, Duloe (via road through Duloe village or direct by fieldpath south-west from Causeland station). Tel: 01503 269007 www.cornishorchards.co.uk Open Tuesday to Saturday, Easter to end October. Farm shop for handcrafted cider (derived from traditional apple varieties such as Cornish Gilliflower and Lord of the Isles) apple juice and wildflower presse. Informal tours if workload permits.

Liskeard

Perambulating Liskeard is like indulging in a virtual game of Snakes & Ladders, so steeply graded are its streets. No one would pretend it's the prettiest town in Cornwall but it has its moments, notably the substantial parish church of St Martin and the Italianate Guildhall dating from the middle of the 19th century when Liskeard's prosperity was at its zenith on account of the copper mines of Caradon and the granite quarries of Cheesewring. Nowadays commerce centres round its twice-weekly cattle market.

Accommodation
PENCUBITT COUNTRY HOUSE HOTEL - Lamellion, Tel: 01579 342694. www.pencubitt.com Victorian house in own grounds within 5 minutes walk west of Liskeard station on road down to Coombe.

Eating & Drinking
THE OLD STAG - adjacent Liskeard station. Tel: 01579 342280. Friendly pub handily located for rail travellers and on the Looe Valley Rail Ale Trail.

Shopping
Liskeard's hilly town centre lies a disconcerting (though see Buses) quarter of an hour's walk north of the railway station. There are banks, new and secondhand bookshops and a branch of PENGELLY'S the fishmongers in the Market Hall. A bustling Farmer's Market is held on the 1st Saturday in the month. In the town centre there's a SOMERFIELD supermarket and a larger branch of SAFEWAY on the eastern edge of the town adjacent to the A38.

Places to Visit
TOURIST INFORMATION - Pike Street. Tel: 01579 349148.
LISKEARD MUSEUM - Pike Street. Tel: 01579 345407.

Connections
TAXIS - Caradon Cars, Tel: 01579 340007.
BUSES - half-hourly service Mon-Sat to/from town centre operated by DAC Coaches (Tel: 01822 834571) who also link Liskeard with the now train-less towns of Bodmin and Callington.

Looe

Superficially a fully paid up member of the British seaside's 'kiss-me-quick' brigade, Looe eschews total vulgarity by virtue of its picturesque setting, the beauty of its small but perfectly formed beach, the continued presence of its fishing fleet and its status as the headquarters of the Shark Fishing Club of Great Britain.

Accommodation
TREHAVEN MANOR HOTEL - Station Road. Tel: 01503 262028 www.trehavenhotel.co.uk
RIVERCROFT HOTEL - Station Road. Tel: 01503 262251 www.rivercrofthotel.co.uk Inexpensive family hotel with family apartments to let handy for station.

Eating & Drinking
TRAWLERS ON THE QUAY - The Quay. Tel: 01503 263593 www.trawlersrestaurant.co.uk Gourmet dinners served Tuesdays to Saturdays in well-appointed surroundings overlooking the harbour.
MAWGAN'S - Higher Market Street. Tel: 01503 365331 www.mawgans.co.uk Lunch on Saturdays and Sundays, dinner from Thursday through to Tuesday. Quality cooking of fresh, locally-sourced produce.
SMUGGLER'S COTT - Higher Market Street. Tel: 01503 262397. Large portions of seafood and steaks render this long-established restaurant perennially popular.
DAVE'S DINER - The Quay. Tel: 01503 262351. Award-winning fish & chips and/or Cornish pasties, eat in or take-away, though beware envious seagulls.

JOLLY SAILOR - Princes Square, West Looe. Tel: 01503 263387. Take the foot-ferry at high tide across the river to sample Doom Bar and pub grub in the oldest pub in Looe dating from 1516.
TRELEAVENS - Fore Street. Ice cream parlour dispensing freshly-made Cornish ice creams of bewildering flavours.

Shopping
Make a bee-line for PENGELLY'S fishmongers on The Quay, as recommended by Rick Stein, and where evidence of the freshness of the fish is guaranteed by the close proximity of the fishmarket and neighbouring fishmerchants premises. Elsewhere the town all too easily gives way to the temptation to cater for the British public's baser seaside instincts, but then somewhere has to do it!

Things to Do
TOURIST INFORMATION - Fore Street. Tel: 01503 262072.
SOUTH EAST CORNWALL DISCOVERY CENTRE - Millpool, West Looe. Tel: 01503 262777
THE OLD GUILDHALL MUSEUM - Tel: 01503 263709. Local history displays featuring Looe's fishing, boat-building and smuggling heritage.

Connections
TAXIS - LOOE TAXIS, Station Road, Tel: 01503 262405.
BUSES - HAMBLYS operate a fairly regular Monday to Saturday service to the picturesque old fishing port of Polperro - Tel: 01503 220660; and FIRST link Polperro with Looe and Plymouth via the Torpoint Ferry also two or three times a day, Tel: 01209 719988.

St Keyne

Wayside halt made famous by its proximity to Paul Corin's museum of music machines and the well said to bestow mastery in marriage to whichever member of the couple drinks its waters first.

Accommodation, Eating & Drinking
THE WELL HOUSE - country house restaurant and hotel adjacent to St Keyne's Well, less than 10 minutes stroll south-west of the station. Tel: 01579 342001 www.wellhouse.co.uk

Places to Visit
MAGNIFICENT MUSIC MACHINES - adjacent railway station. Tel: 01579 343108. Open Easter to end October 10.30am to 5pm. Well commended museum of musical monsters founded by the present owner's father whose own father was a music hall star. Cinema organs, Belgian cafe organs, Mighty Wurlitzers and player pianos lovingly restored and maintained in the atmospheric surroundings of an old watermill.

Sandplace

Derived its name, quite literally, from where the canal barges discharged their cargoes of sand and seaweed consigned to improve the qualities of the local soil.

Accommodation, Eating & Drinking
POLRAEN COUNTRY HOUSE HOTEL - Tel: 01503 263956 www.polraen.co.uk 18th century coaching inn now providing comfortable accommodation within a couple of minutes walk of Sandplace station. Also open to non-residents in the evenings (except Sunday) and on the Rail Ale Trail.

The Atlantic Coast Line

One of the Great Scenic Railways of Devon & Cornwall

THE ATLANTIC COAST LINE

wessextrains

Connecting People, Connecting Places

NOT two miles north-east of the 'world's largest greenhouse' - more widely known as the hugely popular Eden Project - lies the Luxulyan Valley. Watered by the Par River, and densely wooded with deciduous trees, it is a forgotten landscape, as post-industrial in its way as the Eden Project in its clay mined crater, but lacking the latter's millions of visitors. Popularity is an unreliable barometer. Who sees more of the real Cornwall, the global garden-seekers of Eden, or the passenger in the single unit diesel which forms the low season Par to Newquay local on *The Atlantic Coast Line*?

'There was nothing in the world more restful; the train seemed like the highest stage of civilisation.' - the Par to Newquay line certainly found favour with Paul Theroux when he made the journey in 1982*. The railway, he averred, did nothing to alter or spoil the landscape, and the train upon it was 'a gentle machine'. Those who love railways for their own sake will heartily concur. Those who see them as merely a mode of transport might be pleasantly surprised were they to make their way to Par and take the next train to Newquay.

PAR has most of the attributes of a classic railway junction, and there are surprisingly few stations of which that can be said left intact. Newquay trains depart from the outer face of the up island platform. If it is raining you can take shelter under a slate-roofed, timber-valanced, iron-columned canopy that looks as if it has been transmogrified from the illustrations for a *Thomas the Tank Engine* story. At the southern extremity of this platform a lengthy timber and brick built signal box (dating from 1879 - the oldest in Cornwall) controls a welcome plethora of lower quadrant semaphore signals - pure Great Westernry personified!

Constrained by the sharpness of the curve which loops the line through a hundred and eighty degrees, Newquay trains make a cautious departure, picking their way gingerly round the bend to St Blazey. Here are sidings and a depot for the English, Welsh & Scottish Railway Company (EWS) who operate the freight trains which serve the clay industry in these parts so effectively. Such activities go back a long way to a complex background history of mineral lines and tramways built piecemeal in the middle of the 19th century to carry metals, ores and clays down to the ports at Par, Fowey and Newquay. You will be following the course of these pioneering routes for much of your coast to coast journey.

St Blazey is prized amongst railway *cognoscenti* for its roundhouse, erected by the Cornwall Minerals Railway in 1874 to house its original stud of locomotives, uniquely designed for working back to back in pairs as a means of coping with steep gradients in the vicinity. Used by diesel locomotives until as recently as 1987, the roundhouse covered nine 'roads' radiating from a turntable in a style more commonly found on the Continent, British roundhouses being more usually fully covered-in. Disappointingly, nowadays EWS maintain their rolling stock and motive power in the former wagon works and the roundhouse is sub-let as industrial units.

The signalman emerges from St Blazey box to hand your driver the token for the single line section. You can still see the platforms of St Blazey station, closed in 1925 with the abandonment of public passenger services over the line to Fowey. Skirting

The Kingdom by the Sea

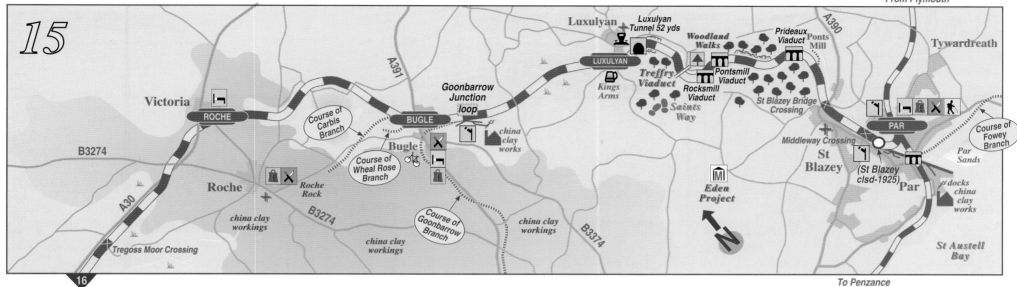

the back of St Blazey town - and passing in the process, Blaise Park, home of St Blazey FC, founded 1896 'Come on you Saints' - the train negotiates a pair of automated level crossings prior to breaking out into open country, the River Par on one side and the old Par Canal on the other, creating the illusion of a causeway.

An overgrown siding disappears into the undergrowth. Not so long ago the Royal Train was regularly stabled overnight in this quiet spot when the Prince of Wales was visiting his Duchy of Cornwall estates. Abruptly, by Ponts Mill, the line leaves the valley floor and commences climbing steeply at 1 in 40, essaying a twisting course through beautiful woodland. It appears profoundly peaceful and inviolate, this mask of trees, but here, in the 19th century, was a hive of industry, all part of Squire Treffry's commercial empire: kilns, water-powered machinery, and an inclined plane which carried a tramway up to the top of the ridge. And most impressive of all, Cornwall's first stone built viaduct, 650 feet long and almost 100 feet high, ten proud arches carrying not only Treffry's tramway but also leats bringing water down from the moors to power the machinery.

Of Amazonian density now, the woods disguise the scars, and as time goes by it is becoming increasingly difficult to find a viewpoint that places Treffry's viaduct in the full

context of its splendour: through the windows of the wheel-screeching train it is possible to blink and miss its looming presence entirely. You would do better to alight at Luxulyan and walk back through the woods to discover this fossilised survivor, as imposing as any Inca temple. Why, you can even walk across the top of it now, imagining yourself the handler of a horse-drawn train of mineral wagons bound for the harbour at Par. Treffry's Coat of Arms embellishes each side of the viaduct which was completed in three years from the laying of the foundation stone on 15th March 1839. On the north side a Latin inscription reads Dum Deo Placuerit - While God Will - and the structure's permanence in the landscape, concealed or not, suggests that 'He' still does.

Sheer, rocky cuttings herald the fairy grotto that is Luxulyan Tunnel. Two hundred and eighty six miles from Paddington, LUXULYAN might as well be on another planet. It is very tempting to get out and melt into this delicious landscape. But before your conscience can ratify the impulse, the train renews its journey, palpably relieved of the responsibility of climbing so steeply, and surging forward into an at first deceptively rural area.

All is not as it seems, however, for the wild, empty aspect framed by the carriage window is soon replaced by the jagged scars of china clay workings. The train hoots mournfully as

if seeking to reassure itself, putting a brave face on its passage through a landscape which has been likened to the Moon. Presently the line doubles and the driver exchanges the token that has ensured your safe progress from St Blazey with the signalman at Goonbarrow Junction, an isolated signal box overshadowed by a huge china clay works with busy sidings.

A 'staff' is issued for the next leg of the journey, providing your train with sole possession of the line between Goonbarrow and Newquay. In the vicinity of BUGLE three separate branches left the main line to provide access into the china clay district. Rationalisation saw them all disused by the end of the 1980s, rendering extinct anachronistic scenes of powerful diesel locomotives, such as the English Electric Class 50s, hauling short trains of elderly four-wheeled wagons along overgrown lines to reach remote clay dries.

Heading disconcertingly in a north-westerly direction, the train proceeds from Bugle to Roche - pithy place names that seem entirely appropriate in this alien landscape. In fact there are overtones of Anglesey - that same sense of ugly beauty. The otherwise bare platform at ROCHE is embellished by a quaint timber shelter which looks as if it has escaped from a Hornby train set. The railway first crosses, then runs alongside the A30: strange bedfellows this traffic-bloated trunk road and the quietly unassuming branch line.

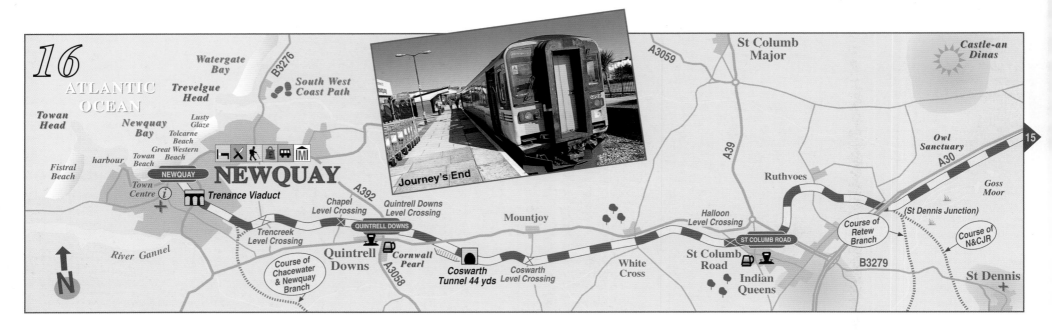

16

ATLANTIC OCEAN

Towan Head

Newquay Bay

Watergate Bay

Trevelgue Head

South West Coast Path

Lusty Glaze
Tolcarne Beach
Great Western Beach
Towan Beach

Fistral Beach

harbour

NEWQUAY

NEWQUAY

Town Centre

Trenance Viaduct

River Gannel

N

Chapel Level Crossing

QUINTRELL DOWNS

Trencreek Level Crossing

Quintrell Downs

Course of Chacewater & Newquay Branch

Cornwall Pearl

Coswarth Tunnel 44 yds

Coswarth Level Crossing

Quintrell Downs Level Crossing

A392

A3058

Mountjoy

White Cross

Journey's End

A3059

A39

St Columb Major

Ruthvoes

Halloon Level Crossing

ST COLUMB ROAD

St Columb Road

Indian Queens

Castle-an Dinas

Owl Sanctuary

A30

Goss Moor

(St Dennis Junction)

Course of Retew Branch

Course of N&CJR

B3279

St Dennis

15

SUMMIT surmounted, the train bowls down to cross Goss Moor, a wild, uncultivated land once, according to legend, hunted over by King Arthur. On the northern horizon Castle-an-Dinas catches the eye, an Iron age fortress built on the site of even older Bronze Age burial mounds. Seven hundred feet above sea level, this was a naturally strategic position commanding ancient trade routes. Evidence suggests that the fortress was occupied between 400BC and 150AD, which rather places the one hundred and fifty year old railway firmly in its historic context.

Southwards, in contrast, the countryside extends to a serrated horizon of spoil heaps and the clutter of china clay workings. A foreground of scrub and bog provides the source of the River Fal. This section of the line was once double track as far as St Dennis Junction. Merely wasteland remains of this once busy railway interchange. You need to seek out old photographs to do it justice. In John Vaughan's comprehensive *The Newquay Branch* (OPC - 1991) an evocative R. C. Riley photograph depicts a Hall class locomotive leaning into the curve as it traverses the main line, whilst Prairie and Pannier tanks busily assemble mineral trains on the Newquay & Cornwall Junction line to Burngullow and the Retew branch respectively. A signal box, lower

quadrants, telegraph poles and tablet catcher add vitality to the view against a fascinating backdrop of conical clay spoil tips, much whiter and more lunar than they are these days. Nothing stands still, however, and wind farms now provide new interest to the view, like them or loath them.

Proposals were made in 1987 to re-route Newquay services over the Newquay & Cornwall Junction line between St Dennis Junction and the Penzance line at Burngullow to the west of St Austell. It was not a route that had ever been used by passenger trains, but it was argued that it would be shorter and quicker. The beauty of the plan also appealed to the highways authority who would be able to demolish the bottle-neck road bridge spanning the A30 near Roche. Though British Rail never any further with it, the scheme lies enshrined in the County Council's 30-year 'Vision'.

The railway arcs past Ruthvoes, deviating from the original course of Treffry's tramway which cut out the loop by passing through a tunnel on a more direct alignment. However the tunnel provided insufficient clearance when the line was converted from horse to steam power in 1874, and the Cornish Minerals Railway felt it was easier to avoid it altogether rather than attempt to widen it out.

Originally called Halloon, the Great Western Railway

renamed the next stop ST COLUMB ROAD when they took over operation of the line. Rarely embarrassed by intervening mileage, the GWR took the name from St Columb Major, a three mile hike to the north. A new shelter has recently gone in here, evidence that the modern railway *does* care, whatever the apparent paucity of custom on offer. These days the up platform remains in use, though the down is still evident, last used in 1965 before the loop and the goods yard and the signal box were dismantled.

Helicopters, exercising over St Mawgan airfield fill the skies and there are civilian aircraft using Newquay Airport to be spotted as well. The countryside becomes kinder, sustaining crops and cattle. There is another wind farm to the south on Newlyn Downs. You begin to sense an end to your journey, though so diminutive are some of the little granite overbridges on this section of the line that you wonder if the train will manage to squeeze under them. Covered in lichen and ivy, they appear almost to have sprouted organically out of the earth.

A deep cutting leads to Coswarth Tunnel, and an equally dank stretch of line ensues before the railway passes under the A392 and reaches QUINTRELL DOWNS, the penultimate stop, always assuming that anyone wishes to alight or board.

Mostly, the only activity prevalent here now is of a Friesian herd contentedly munching the grass beyond the platform fence.

The train lopes into Newquay like a runner approaching the finishing line with no personal best to beat and nothing to prove. The sea remains obstinately out of view. Scrubland makes it difficult to ascertain the course of the short-lived Chacewater to Newquay line, opened in 1905 and abandoned fifty-eight years later. It was largely responsible for the development of Perranporth as a resort. St Agnes was another stop. A section of the route has been adapted for use by the narrow gauge Lappa Valley Railway. Tolcarn was a triangular junction and came in handy for turning tender engines, sometimes *whole* trains if they were too lengthy in the holiday season to be conveniently run-round at the terminus.

Trenance Viaduct (twice rebuilt from Treffry's original spindly timber structure, locally known as 'The Spider') allows trains to make something of 'an entrance' into Newquay.

Misleadingly triumphant, for there is a paucity of grandeur surrounding the station now. Just seagulls calling plaintively over the rooftops. Whilst there is a chastening inevitability about the fact that a supermarket occupies the bulk of the station site. At least the lengthy single platform is still capable of handling the long distance trains which ply the branch on summer weekends, and at least you have the satisfaction of ticking off another West Country branch line, 'done and dusted'. By all means patronise the fabulous Eden Project - millions can't be wrong. But give this entertaining railway ride a fling as well. The carriage windows encompass a tasty slice of real Cornwall.

Gazetteer

Bugle
Map 15

Working village deep in china clay country, said to derive its name from the sound of the old coaching horns being blown as they passed through.

Eating Drinking & Accommodation
BUGLE INN - Fore Street. Tel: 01726 850307 www.bugleinn.co.uk CAMRA recommended stone-built inn at centre of village 3 or 4 minutes walk from the station. Food and accommodation, St Austell ales. Breakfasts available for non-residents.

Shopping
SPAR stores just up from the railway station. Cash machine.

Connections
BICYCLE HIRE - Bugle Cycle Hire. Tel: 01726 852285. Cycle to the Eden Project - or anywhere else for that matter.

Luxulyan
Map 15

A cosy village of granite cottages and modern infills. The substantial parish church of St Ciricius and Julitta is worth visiting. But the best reason for getting out at Luxulyan is to walk down the wooded valley to pay homage to Joseph Treffry's astonishing viaduct/aqueduct.

Eating & Drinking
KING'S ARMS - Tel: 01726 850202. Comfortable, well-appointed pub a couple of minutes walk from the station. Food (except Monday evenings) and St Austell ales.

Shopping
Small post office stores to north of station.

Walking
Luxulyan is on the Saints Way which crosses Cornwall from Padstow to Fowey. The station also provides access to enjoyable woodland walks in the Luxulyan Valley.

Newquay
Map 16

Once you have encountered its beaches you can forgive Newquay anything. Sands and surf redeem all sins, and you find your preconceptions and prejudices evaporating as readily as the spume. The 'New Kaye' in question dates from the 15th century and for four hundred years Newquay was little more or less than a pilchard fishing harbour, the bulk of each catch being exported to France or Italy. The whitewashed Huer's Hut, from which a watch was kept for pilchard shoals, remains enderingly intact on a headland above the harbour. With the advent of passenger trains the town reinvented itself as a resort, burgeoning to become Cornwall's largest. When road transport gained the upper hand Newquay might have gone the tawdry way of many English seaside resorts, but in recent years the growth of surfing has given it a new lease of life.

Accommodation
THE HEADLAND HOTEL - Fistral Beach. Tel: 01637 872211 www.headlandhotel.co.uk Iconic clifftop hotel with terracotta trimmings.
WHIPSIDERRY HOTEL - Porth. Tel: 01637 874777. Two star hotel in idyllic setting to north of town centre.
FISTRAL BACKPACKERS - Headland Road. Tel: 01637 873146 www.fistralbackpackers.co.uk

Eating & Drinking
TAD & NICKS - Fore Street. Tel: 01637 874868 www.tadnnicks.co.uk Internet cafe.
FISTRAL BLU - Fistral Beach. Tel: 01637 878782 www.fistral-blu.co.uk Much vaunted upstairs, downstairs cafe/restaurant in peerless setting overlooking the Atlantic Ocean.
FINNS RESTAURANT - South Quay Hill. Tel: 01637 874062 www.finnscafe.com 'Al fresco' eating on the harbour's edge.

Shopping
Surfing chic - both practical and purely ornamental - is Newquay's stock in trade. Elsewhere, excellent pasties from Peter Morris on East Street and cream cakes from Wilbur's on Fore Street.

Things to Do
TOURIST INFORMATION - Marcus Hill. Tel: 01637 854020 www.newquay.co.uk
TUNNELS THROUGH TIME - St Michaels Road. Tel: 01637 873379 Waxwork displays of Cornwall's lurid past.
BLUE REEF AQUARIUM - Towan Beach. Tel: 01637 878134 www.bluereefaquarium.co.uk Colourful fish, etc. in tanks.
NEWQUAY ZOO - Tel: 01637 873342 www.newquayzoo.co.uk Wild animals, etc. in captivity.
LAPPA VALLEY STEAM RAILWAY - St Newlyn East. Tel: 01872 510317 www.lappavalley.co.uk Narrow gauge steam trains operating along a short length of the former GWR Chacewater & Newquay line.
ROUTE 500 - Tel: 01637 871871. Open top vintage double-decker bus tours of Newquay. Late May to late September daily (ex Saturday) departing the bus station at 20 minutes past the hour from 09.20 to 17.20. Nearest stop to the railway station by the Great Western Hotel - turn right out of station onto Cliff Road.

Connections
BUSES - useful links with Padstow and Truro etc. Tel: 0870 608 2 608.
TAXIS - Bluebird Taxis. Tel: 01637 852222.
BICYCLE HIRE - Shoreline Gifts, Fore Street. Tel: 01637 879165.

Walking
South West Coast Path.

Par
Map 15

Railhead for St Blazey and Quiller-Couch's 'Troy Town', or Fowey if you prefer.

Eating Drinking & Accommodation
ROYAL INN -Tel: 01726815601. Friendly family pub overlooking the station. Food and accommodation. Sharp's and Skinner's Cornish beers. CAMRA recommended.
VAL'S PLACE - Fish & chips and home-made pasties. On the A3082 to south of station by railway bridge.

Shopping
SPAR store (5 minutes walk east of station) with hot take-away food counter. Chemist, newsagents and post office.

Things to Do
The docks - like all docks everywhere, sadly - are out of bounds to casual visitors, but they can't stop you walking on the wide sands and watching the coming and going of the clay 'boats'.

Connections
BUSES - half hourly, Mon-Sat, hourly Sun connections from Par station to Fowey. Tel: 0870 608 2 608.

Quintrell Downs
Map 16

A pub, a post office stores, a pearl jewellery outlet and possibly the busiest road roundabout in Cornwall.

Things to Do
CORNWALL PEARL - Tel: 01637 872991. 'Wander through Cornwall's World of Pearls' and buy some at the end. Guided tours and refreshments. Open daily 9.30am - 5.30pm. Across the road from the railway station.

Roche
Map 15

The station is located in Victoria, a mile to the north of the old mining and quarrying centre of Roche. Roche Rock is famous for the ruined chapel on its jagged summit and hermit's cell below. The parish church rejoices in the name of St Gonandus.

Eating, Drinking & Accommodation
VICTORIA INN - Travel lodge style accommodation close to the railway station and mainly catering for tired and exasperated motorists on the A30. Tel: 01726 890207.

Shopping
Co-op, bakery and pharmacy in the centre of Roche; plus fish & chips and two more pubs.

St Columb Road
Map 16

Station for St Columb Major three miles to the north and for the much closer and quaintly named former mining village of Indian Queens to the south.

Eating & Drinking
Basic boozer called the QUEEN & RAILWAY (Tel: 01726 860343) to the south of the station. In Indian Queens there is a fish & chip shop/restaurant called PORT & STARBOARD (Tel: 01726 860276).

Things to Do
The SCREECH OWL SANCTUARY (Tel: 01726 860182 www.owlsanct.freeserve.co.uk) lies a two mile walk east of the railway station and is home to over a hundred and forty owls and birds of prey from all over the world. Refreshments available.

The Maritime Line

One of the Great Scenic Railways of Devon & Cornwall

THE MARITIME LINE

wessextrains

Connecting People, Connecting Places

JOHN LOUGHBOROUGH PEARSON'S retro-Gothic cathedral draws the eye as trains from the north put on their brakes, crossing a pair of lofty viaducts on their approach to Truro's typically Great Western station. The artist Stanhope Alexander Forbes must have seen the cathedral in the process of being built (it was begun in 1880 and completed in 1909) when he reached here from Paddington in 1884, reconnoitring Cornwall for fresh inspiration. Finally found, not in Falmouth, as he had imagined might be the case, but in St Ives.

Forbes's train would have been broad gauge then, and on his journey through Devon and Cornwall he would have crossed many of Isambard Kingdom Brunel's trademark timber viaducts. Brunel employed wood to save costs. The promoters of the West Country's railways realistically did not envisage the traffics and profits being experienced in more heavily industrialised areas of the country. In his 1957 biography of Brunel, L. T. C. Rolt describes how the engineer perfected a standardised timber viaduct design of 'great beauty and simplicity'. Essentially each viaduct comprised a number of stone piers on top of which two sets of four timber beams fanned out to support the main longitudinal timbers which carried the track. Cross and diagonal ties added considerable strength to the structure. 'A simpler or more graceful design or one better calculated to become part of the *genius loci* of the region would be hard to conceive' Rolt waxed lyrically, adding that the tapering pillars of local stone looked as much at home in the 'primeval, storm-bitten landscape of western Cornwall' as the gaunt chimney stacks of the tin mines.

Nowadays we would think of the timber viaducts almost in organic terms, deeply regretting their loss. The Falmouth line boasted eight of them, including two of the last to be replaced by full masonry structures, Carnon and Collegewood. The Great Western Railway set about a rolling programme to replace the timber viaducts towards the end of the 19th century. Brunel had employed a specialised yellow pine from the Baltic, cheap enough to acquire at the time, but increasingly difficult to obtain as time went on. A spar might enjoy a reliable working life of thirty years. Bridge gangs examined each viaduct on a quarterly basis, replacing timbers where and when deemed necessary by skilfully lowering themselves on ropes from the top of the bridge like the egg collectors of Bempton Cliffs in East Yorkshire, or, more pertinently perhaps, the abseiling engineers of Dawlish and Teignmouth today.

With such images jostling your imagination, you can take your present-day place on *The Maritime Line* diesel unit in Truro's No.1 bay platform and prepare yourself for the twelve mile journey down to Falmouth. The line you are about to travel on opened in 1863, built to broad gauge dimensions by the Cornwall Railway as the last section of a through route from Plymouth. Ironically, Falmouth had been anticipating the arrival of the Railway Age for some thirty years prior to this. Rival schemes having flourished and withered in promoters eternally optimistic bosoms. Falmouth, it was felt, needed a railway to safeguard its status as a packet port in the face of competition with Southampton. Parliament took sides: Whigs supporting the concept of a 'central' route from Exeter via Launceston whilst Tories favoured a 'coastal' line. Typically, as a result there was more talk than action. Time lends enchantment to such shenanigans, but aren't we experiencing exactly the same frustrations and protractions in the 21st century *vis-a-vis* the modern railway's role in public transport and the nature of its post-privatisation structure?

Probably having provided connections with trains on the main line, the Falmouth branch train pulls out past the sizeable premises of Cornwall Farmers which occupy the site of Truro's motive power depot, coded 83F by British Railways Western Region and host to a modest allocation of Granges, Manors, Prairies and Panniers in steam days. The preserved steam locomotives *Erlestoke Manor* and *Dinmore Manor* were both at one time Truro engines.

Soon after departing, the Falmouth train plunges into Highertown Tunnel, unusual at one time for containing the broad gauge track of the Cornwall Railway and the standard gauge track of the West Cornwall Railway side by side. The cutting into which you emerge was the location of the West Cornwall Railway's original Truro terminus.

At Penwithers Junction the Falmouth train leaves the Penzance line. Until 1971 this was something of a railway cross-roads, for in addition to the Penzance and Falmouth lines a branch led round to Newham at the head of the Truro River. Originally this was laid by the West Cornwall Railway to provide Truro with a more accessible terminus than Highertown. But by 1859 this had been superseded by a new through station, and for virtually all of the remainder of its surprisingly extended life the Newham Branch was used for goods only, notably in later years to provide access for coal trains to Truro's gas works.

You can descry the trackbed of the Newham line curving melancholically away from Penwithers as the train negotiates a high embankment which replaced Penwithers Viaduct in 1926. In some instances it was considered easier and more cost-effective to infill the smaller ravines spanned by timber viaducts than build replacement masonry structures. There was also a Penwithers Viaduct on the Penzance line. It was rebuilt in 1887 and you can see its masonry arches from the right hand side of the train.

The Falmouth line's Penwithers Viaduct had been ninety feet high, so you can imagine the amount of spoil which needed to be deposited to form the embankment which took its place. At the time this must have been a raw gash in the landscape. Now it is so overgrown by vegetation that it isn't entirely apparent that you are on an

embankment at all. Indeed, thirty or forty years ago the overriding image retained from a journey on the Falmouth branch was of Cornwall's characteristically crumpled landscape. Now, however, the unchecked growth of lineside vegetation creates an altogether different impression, more that of a West Country lane, overhung by deep green 'tunnels' of trees.

What has not changed is the once familiar and now to be treasured clickety-clack of the wheels resounding over jointed track. Another embankment carries you over the site of Ringwell Viaduct replaced in 1933 before you breast one of this roller-coaster line's four summits and sink into a deep cutting on the approach to Sparnock Tunnel. By midsummer, foxgloves have replaced the primroses in such cuttings, making successive journeys over the line rewarding whatever the time of year.

Carnon Viaduct was rebuilt in 1933. The piers of the timber viaduct can be clearly seen from the right-hand side of the train. They also appear in S. J. 'Lamorna' Birch's evocative painting of the viaduct entitled *The Holiday, Carnon Valley* which depicts a group of children at play in meadowland as a steam train crosses the viaduct beyond. Birch was one of the artists attracted to Cornwall in the wake of Stanhope Forbes, becoming a father figure to the Newlyn School of *en plein air* painters. Another of his paintings depicts the tin dressing plant at Bissoe. He died in his adopted county in 1955. The scene of *The Holiday* can be savoured still - albeit not with steam - by cyclists and walkers on a public trail developed from the long abandoned trackbed of the Redruth & Chasewater Railway, a four foot gauge, initially horse-drawn, line opened down to Devoran in 1826. Devoran today evinces the atmosphere of a lost port. Large quantities of tin and copper were shipped from here throughout the 19th century.

The generous proportions of the overbridges arches recall the line's broad gauge origins. One good example precedes the first stop at PERRANWELL which retains a cast iron 'running in' nameboard, together with a modern vernacular shelter of the sort used on both the *Tamar Valley* and *Looe Valley* lines. The solid looking goods shed has survived to find use with a scaffolding company. But, sadly, the handsome elevated signal box which spanned one of the sidings has been demolished.

From Plymouth

17

Buckshead Tunnel 320 yds

A39

A390

Truro Viaduct
Carvedras Viaduct

river cruises

Malpas

TRURO

City Centre

TRURO

harbour

Truro River

Highertown Tunnel 70yds

A390

County Hall

Course of Newham Branch

Penwithers Junction

Penwithers Viaduct

site of viaduct

To Penzance

site of viaduct

Playing Place

B3289

Sparnock Tunnel 491 yds

Come to Good

Carnon Downs

Coast to Coast Trail

Bissoe

Carnon River

Carnon Viaduct

Devoran

harbour

Perranwell

PERRANWELL

Course of Redruth & Chasewater Railway

Royal Oak

A39

River Kennal

N

Perran Viaduct

Perranworthal

18

IN common with the *Avocet Line*, the *Maritime Line* is very much a commuter line in addition to being a scenic railway sought after by tourists. This lends it an invigorating verisimilitude not always present where a line survives only for fun. When Paul Atterbury travelled over the route searching for copy for his *End of the Line* in 1994, he enjoyed sharing the journey with schoolchildren, young mothers and their babes, elderly people and others in 'that indefinable category known broadly as professional'. Students are regular users of the line as well, though sadly perhaps, no longer sailors. For many years the Great Western Railway laid on through trains or portions to Paddington and there were boat trains on occasion. But in most respects the Truro to Falmouth line was worked as a branch, Prairie and Pannier tanks providing the motive power in steam days.

Beyond Perranwell (Map 17) the train skips exuberantly downhill to cross Perran Viaduct (rebuilt 1927) before climbing again and sounding its horn on the approach to Perran Tunnel. Ponsanooth Viaduct (rebuilt 1930) rapidly follows and then embankments carry you over the sites of vanished viaducts called Pascoe and Penryn which sound as if they might have been a Falmouth dental practice.

The original station at PENRYN was moved sideways in 1922 to ease the line's curvature and provide more siding space. An extensive car park occupies the site of the old platforms and a car auction mart stands where the goods yard was once full of cattle wagons and coal trucks. It was a busy yard but somehow or other space was found for a pair of camping coaches in the 1930s. From the southern end of the station the line falls steeply at 1 in 59. In contrast, the old goods headshunt ran along the top of a retaining wall on the level. The wall is still evident beneath a high, wide-arched road bridge, encouraging you to picture the days when a Prairie tank might be snorting up and down the sidings, sorting out the wagons - a far cry from the Tuesday and Friday evening car auctions of the present day.

Leaving Penryn the train crosses Collegewood Viaduct, the last of Brunel's West Country timber viaducts to be rebuilt in 1934. What a shame that it couldn't have been preserved. Had it been so it would undoubtably have been a huge attraction today. Over three hundred yards long, at its highest point it was over a hundred feet above the valley floor. Concrete blocks were used in the building of the new masonry arched

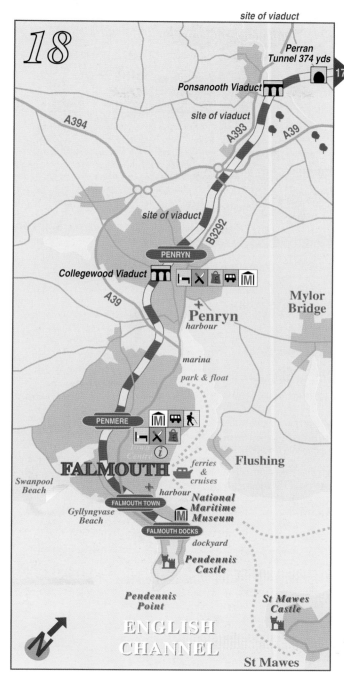

bridge. All this fine historical detail is probably lost on the average traveller, though one hopes that at least they might be admiring the panoramic view over Penryn, its clock-towered town hall a prominent feature against the backdrop of a creek picturesquely filled with yacht masts.

From three hundred feet above sea level in the vicinity of Sparnock (Map 17) the railway descends almost to the datum level at Falmouth. Its entry into the port is surreptitious and suburban, but so dense is the lineside vegetation, all you see of the houses which jostle the line are roof tiles and the occasional dormer window like a raised eyebrow.

PENMERE is a pretty platform tenderly groomed by the Friends of Penmere Station, a small band of railway enthusiasts and gardeners formed in 1993 to reverse years of unstaffed neglect. Their's is a good example of what can be achieved with volunteer enthusiasm, adding weight to the Community Rail Partnership premise that branch line railways can effectively foster environmental benefits and embrace social inclusion. Looking at this neat suburban station now, it's hard to envisage that there was a rail-connected Ministry of Defence oil depot here between 1940 and 1971.

FALMOUTH TOWN station opened as recently as 1970, though this is its third title, having previously been known as Falmouth and later The Dell. During the period it was simply called Falmouth it constituted the end of the line as far as passenger services were concerned, though trains were required to run as empty stock down to Falmouth Docks before reversing for safety reasons. There are no such complications now, for Falmouth Docks re-opened in 1975. If you sense that a large proportion of the people on Falmouth Town platform seem disinterested in boarding the train - and lack the eccentric look of railway enthusiasts - the explanation is that they are Truro-bound and merely waiting patiently for the train to run down to the terminus to reverse. Sometimes the more footsore or baggage weary will board anyway, grateful to sit down.

And so to the end of the line. Sadly diminished, like many branch line termini, FALMOUTH DOCKS retains a lengthy canopy with a curiously rounded roof, the only surviving remnant of a once imposing station with a handsome overall roof. The extensive dockyard railway - shunted by steam as recently as 1986 - lies beneath brambles, all hopes that Falmouth might develop as a container port apparently abandoned.

Gazetteer

Falmouth
Map 18

After Sydney and Rio de Janeiro, Falmouth is the third deepest natural harbour in the world, and one might happily spend weeks unravelling its rich maritime history and savouring its splendid watery setting. Moreover, Falmouth is visibly emerging from a period of inertia, touting itself as a port of call for cruise liners, and energised by being the choice for an offshoot of the National Maritime Museum.

Accommodation
GROVE HOTEL - Grove Place. Tel: 01326 319577 www.thegrovehotel.net Comfortable and inexpensive small hotel opposite National Maritime Museum and less than 10 minutes walk from 'Town' station.
PENMERE MANOR - Tel: 01326 211411. Three star Best Western hotel close to Penmere station.
ST MICHAEL'S HOTEL - Gyllyngvase Beach. Tel: 01326 312707 www.stmichaelshotel.com Stylish three star hotel overlooking beach and close to 'Town' station.

Eating & Drinking
THE GURKHA - The Moor. Atmospheric Nepalese/Indian restaurant. Tel: 01326 311483. The waiters wear national costume.
SEAFARERS RESTAURANT - Arwenack Street. Tel: 01326 319851. Lively, well-appointed, mostly fish restaurant.
HUNKY DORY - Arwenack Street. Tel: 01326 212997. Freshly cooked local produce for dinner in stylish surrounds.
QUAYSIDE INN - Arwenack Street. Tel: 01326 312113. Overlooks the Custom House Quay. Outdoor tables, 'One Pot Pies', and a good choice of Cornish ales.
SEVEN STARS - The Moor. Tel: 01326 312111. Gem of an unspoilt pub (on CAMRA national inventory of historic pub interiors) offering good beer and conversation.

Shopping
It's good to see a sizeable town where the commonplace retail chains are still outnumbered by independent retailers. Too many, alas, to mention by name herein except for DE WYNN'S old-fashioned tea and coffee merchant and the FALMOUTH BOOKSELLER, both excellent in their way and both located on Church Street. Also, a mouthwatering plethora of pasty shops, including CHOAKS on Killigrew Street, OGGY OGGY on Church Street and Arwenack Street, and the CORNISH MINER, Custom House Quay.

Things to Do
TOURIST INFORMATION - Killigrew Street. Tel: 01326 312300 www.go-cornwall.com
NATIONAL MARITIME MUSEUM - Discovery Quay. Tel: 01326 313388 www.nmmc.co.uk 3 minutes walk from 'Docks' station, this splendid offshoot of Greenwich is an interactive museum in the modern manner celebrating our island race's relationship with the sea with particular emphasis on small boats and Cornwall's maritime heritage.

PENDENNIS CASTLE - Castle Drive (less than 10 minutes walk east from 'Docks' station or use Road Train. Tel: 01326 316594 www.english-heritage.org.uk/pendennis Fortress since Henry VIII's time to the Second World War. Panoramic views of Carrick Roads, across which frequent ferries link Falmouth with Pendennis' twin fortress, St Mawes, also open to the public - Tel: 01326 270526.

Boating
To visit Falmouth and not take a boat trip would be like going to Venice and not hiring a gondola. One of the most enjoyable itineraries is operated by Enterprise Boats (Tel: 01326 374241) to/from Truro via the River Fal and King Harry Ferry. Worth combining, perhaps, with the train in one direction. Alternatively, Falmouth Pleasure Cruises (Tel: 01326 211056) operate to/from Helford River and Frenchman's Creek. Further details on www.falriverlinks.co.uk

Walking
South West Coast Path.

Connections
TAXIS - Falmouth & Penryn Radio Taxis. Tel: 01326 315194.
ROAD TRAIN - Tel: 01872 273453. Runs hourly April to October, providing a lively and entertaining way of seeing Falmouth and visiting various attractions. 2004 timings include a stop at 'Docks' station at 28 minutes past the hour.
CYCLE HIRE - Falmouth Bike Shop, Trelawney Road. Tel: 01326 317679.
BUSES - useful connections to coastal and inland settlements the railway doesn't reach. Tel: 0870 608 2 608.
CAR HIRE - Central Garage. Tel: 01326 211227. Less than 5 minutes walk from 'Town' station.

Penryn
Map 18

Tourism has left Penryn largely untouched, leaving it with a not altogether uncongenial scruffiness which affectionately recalls many of France's small towns.

Accommodation
PROSPECT HOUSE - Church Road. Tel: 01326 373198 www.prospecthouse.co.uk Characterful, well-appointed guest accommodation in the former early 19th century home of a Packet Ship captain across the road from the harbour.

Eating & Drinking
Pubs and takeaways - including two good fish & chip shops.

Shopping
Basic needs, two banks (one with cash machine).

Things to Do
PENRYN MUSEUM - Monday to Friday, 10am-3.30pm. Located in former Town Hall with handsome clock tower.

Perranwell
Map 17

Scattered community with fine Nonconformist chapel and easy access to the Mineral Tramways Coast to Coast Trail. Refreshments at the CAMRA recommended Royal Oak (Tel: 01872 863175) 5 minutes walk south-west of the station. Cycle hire (open daily all year) from Bissoe Tramways - Tel: 01872 870341 www.cornwallcyclehire.com

Truro
Map 17

Cornwall's capital city since 1877, waxing as Bodmin waned. Handsome thoroughfares make for enjoyable exploration: Walsingham Place's Georgian crescent; late 18th century Lemon Street's dignified climb from the centre; and wherever you go the high-spired Victorian cathedral looming over the rooftops like a guardian angel.

Accommodation
ROYAL HOTEL - Lemon Street. Tel: 01872 270345 www.royalhotelcornwall.co.uk Johansen recommended.
BAY TREE GUEST HOUSE - Ferris Town. Tel: 01872 240274. Inexpensive guest house accommodation close to the station.

Eating & Drinking
CHARLOTTE'S TEA ROOM - Boscawen Street. Tel: 01872 263706. Elegant first floor tearoom in antiques centre. Aproned waitresses give it a throwback feel.
CAFE CITRON - Lemon Street. Tel: 01872 274144. Informal Mediterranean brasserie.
CITRON VITE - Lemon Street. Tel: 01872 223271. Patisserie, delicatessen and sandwich bar.
SAFFRON - Quay Street. Tel: 01872 263771 www.saffronrestauranttruro.co.uk Campaign for Real Food accredited cafe/restaurant housed in former butchers shop.
WIG & PEN - Frances Street. Tel: 01872 273028. Rail Ale Trail and CAMRA recommended pub on way into town centre from station.

Shopping
An enjoyable centre for shopping - wherever your interests lie. There's a lively PANNIER MARKET on Lemon Quay, whilst nearby LEMON STREET MARKET is a stylish centre housing a fishmongers, bakery, delicatessen, gift shop and gallery. On New Bridge Street INNSPIRED (Tel: 01872 227337) deals in Cornish bottled beers and brewery memorabilia. Two good bookshops: TRURO BOOKSHOP on Frances Street (with a particularly strong railway section! - Tel: 01872 272185) and OTTAKARS (with a Costa coffee shop) on Boscawen Street. On the way back to the station drop into THE CHEESE SHOP on Ferris Town (Tel: 01872 270742) and sample before you purchase some of Cornwall's most mouthwatering handmade cheeses.

Things to Do
TOURIST INFORMATION - Boscawen Street. Tel: 01872 274555 www.info@truro.gov.uk
ROYAL CORNWALL MUSEUM - River Street. Tel: 01872 272205 www.royalcornwallmuseum.org.uk Prestigious repository of Cornish art and history. Excellent shop and cafe.
SKINNER'S BREWERY - Riverside, Newham. Tel: 01872 271885 www.skinnersbrewery.com. Brewery shop and tours by arrangement.

Boating
See Falmouth.

Connections
TAXIS - A2B Taxis. Tel: 01872 272989.
BUSES - Truronian. Tel: 01872 273453.
CAR HIRE - Hertz. Tel: 01872 223638. Office located on station.

The St Ives Bay Line

One of the Great Scenic Railways of Devon & Cornwall

THE ST. IVES BAY LINE

wessextrains

Connecting People, Connecting Places

ONCE it carried pilchards, now it carries people. Whatever is asked of the *St Ives Bay Line* it copes manfully. Why, it even used to deliver lumps of rock for St Ives's resident sculptress, Barbara Hepworth. Indeed, one doubts if St Ives would have developed so readily as a quaint outpost of the arts if the railway had not made getting there so easy from the late 19th century onwards.

In pure railway terms, the St Erth to St Ives branch line is notable for being the last line to be laid to Brunel's broad gauge. First proposals, in 1845, caused riots. The potato crop had failed and it was felt, locally at least, that a railway would rob St Ives of any residual agricultural wealth it might retain. Thirty years later, buoyed by the spectacular growth of the pilchard fishing industry, railway construction was viewed more favourably. The line opened in June 1877, the flag-bedecked first train hauled by an engine called *Elephant*.

For a branch barely over four miles long, the St Ives line punches well above its weight, both scenically and in matters of railway interest and history. ST ERTH is a comparatively unspoilt country junction and is being developed by Wessex Trains as an 'artistic gateway to St Ives', a studio and gallery having been opened in the station. Sometimes it seems as if more passengers disgorge here, out of trains from the north, than proceed to Penzance, a fact which recalls the Great Western Railway's habit of diverting the *Cornish Riviera Express* to St Ives on Summer Saturdays. On such occasions, two chirpy little Prairie tanks would back on to the ten coach train at St Erth, relieve the express locomotive of its responsibilities, and proceed with palpable pride to St Ives, treating passengers along the way to some of the most spectacular coastal scenery to be seen through a carriage window anywhere.

Apart from the occasional through-run from Penzance, the diesel unit for St Ives waits snugly in its self-appointed 'bay', at a slightly lower level than the through platforms, as if marking a spirit of independency. The driver keeps the 'staff' for the branch line, a time-worn 'one-engine-in-steam' guarantee against collision. Prepared to wait realistically on up-country connections, patience is displayed towards tardy passengers. But there is a tide in the affairs of trains when departure is of the essence, and you pull out, past the signal box and under the A30, pacing yourself for four miles of undiluted enjoyment.

The platform at LELANT SALTINGS was opened in 1978, specifically to provide motorists with a 'park & ride' facility that would take pressure off the narrow streets of St Ives. It has been an unqualified success. Witness the crowds who board the train here all summer through. Folk, who probably never experience another railway journey from one year to the next, suddenly appreciate the beneficial effects of train travel. As conversions go, Damascus has nothing on Lelant Saltings. To think that Beeching planned to close this line!

Skirting the bird-rich salt flats of the Hayle estuary, the train calls - on request - at LELANT, a charming timber-built station long-since privately owned, but advertising 'cream teas' in season. The Great Western Railway 'stabled' a camping coach here. In earlier times there was a branch to a riparian wharf. In Vic Mitchell and Keith Smith's nostalgic book *Branch Lines to Falmouth, Helston and St Ives* (Middleton

Press, 2001) there is a poignant reproduction of a Parliamentary Class Emigrant's Ticket from Lelant to Liverpool, price 25 shillings, recalling many a bitter-sweet departure from Cornwall to the New World.

Coast-hugging railways were rarely easy-builds. From virtually water's edge at Lelant, the *St Ives Bay Line* climbs to almost a hundred and fifty feet above sea level at its summit, necessitating a ruling gradient of 1 in 60 together with a sequence of sharp curves. Wheels protesting at such restricted radii, the train assumes a maritime personality as it hugs the shoreline of the River Hayle. You might almost be aboard one of those fishing smacks making their way circumspectly out to sea; 'SS' denoting that the vessel is registered at St Ives of course! At lower states of the tide, keep an eye peeled for egrets - the estuary is an RSPB reserve.

Post industrial Hayle looks intriguing on the far side of the river's narrow, fast-flowing mouth, and you make a mental note to further explore. But such promises are rapidly forgotten as the diesel unit emerges from a cutting to be presented with the full panoply of St Ives Bay in all its considerable splendour, stretching from St Ives Head in the west to Godrevy Point in the east. On Godrevy Island stands the lighthouse that inspired one of Virginia Woolf's most famous works. At low tide the sweep of sands is breathtaking.

Inland - always assuming you can tear your gaze away - and overlooked by St Uny's church, lie the august links of the West Cornwall Golf Course, founded by one of the church's Victorian incumbents, Richard Frederick Tyacke. He was reputedly so keen on the sport that he would play before funerals, keeping a watchful eye from the links until the cortege appeared, then donning his robes of office and fixing an appropriate countenance in a quick sprint across the fairways to greet the mourners. He is buried in the south-east corner of the churchyard with a favourable view over the course.

How the Prairies must have panted up the stiff gradient to the summit just short of Carbis Bay. Clearing the golf course, the railway plunges in rocky cuttings through the Carrack Gladden headland. So recalcitrant proved this rock, that the railway engineers were only too happy to draw upon the expertise of local miners to blast the line's path. A footbridge was erected, spanning the far mouth of the cutting, to provide access to Hawkes Point for the 'huers' employed in keeping a watch for shoals of pilchards. It is still in place today, part

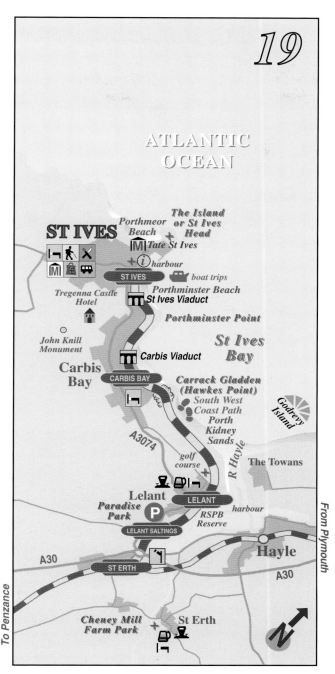

of a network of narrow pathways paralleling the line which provide good vantage points for photographers.

All that remains of the original station at CARBIS BAY is a cast iron kissing gate. The Booking Hall stood at road level above the single platform, more or less where Wessex Trains offer ticket sales from a portacabin on busy days during the season, when many local holidaymakers are sensibly tempted to visit St Ives by train. Hotels and villas and bungalows overlook the wide sweep of sand between the headlands and provide a succinctly illustrated lecture on the development of the British seaside resort. On the beach, stoic behind their windbreaks, the general public make the best of the British weather. But on a hot day, outside the school holidays, Carbis Bay offers all the pleasures of an earthly paradise.

Few pleasures can beat a branch line train, felt the American novelist and travel writer, Paul Theroux, inspired by his journey on the St Ives train*. Travelling in his footsteps, you must be feeling this too, wishing that the journey would last far longer, imagining yourself a potential 'Flying Dutchman' of train travel. Delving into cuttings swarthy with trees, the diesel rounds Porthminster Point, making its way down into ST IVES almost as precipitously as it climbed to Carbis Bay. How the first holidaymakers hearts must have leapt in those early broad gauge days, emerging from the cutting to a view of Porth-minster Sands - no putting green then, but lines of pilchard boats drawn up on the shore. A kick-back siding led to a stolid engine shed. Then came a viaduct, then a goods yard, then the station, a lengthy platform curving invitingly around the contours of the shoreline supported by a substantial granite retaining wall. All the trappings, that is, of an individual, yet quintessential, West Country branch line terminus. A shame, then, that British Rail saw fit, in a 'cost-saving' exercise forty years ago, to cut back the line and demolish the station. Shades of Looe! By all means make track savings to take advantage of the operational simplicities of dieselisation, but why should motorists benefit? Let them use their legs for once. The new platform should have been as close to the town as feasible, not back by the viaduct.

But let's not end on a sour note. We are, as the jargon goes, where we are, and there can be few termini sweeter than St Ives on a sunny day. The seaside brings out the child in us all. Grab your bucket and spade. Last one on to the beach buys the ice creams!

*The Kingdom by the Sea - Hamish Hamilton 1983

Gazetteer

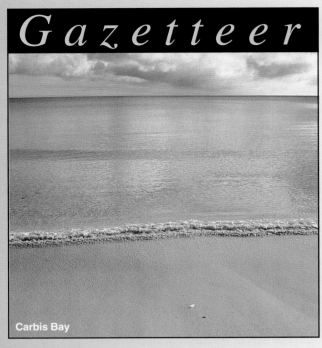

Carbis Bay

Carbis Bay

Archetypal Great Western 'Holiday Haunt' redeveloped in the Edwardian era from a former mining village of which scant evidence remains. Pristine, smooth-sloping sandy beach book-ended by headlands. Plenty of accommodation renders this a peaceful alternative to St Ives. On the South West Coast Path.

Accommodation
CARBIS BAY HOTEL - Tel: 01736 795311 *www.carbisbayhotel.co.uk* Three star hotel established in 1894 and featured in the works of Rosamund Pilcher. 3 minutes downhill from the station. Self-catering properties also available.
BOSKERISS HOTEL - Tel: 01736 796297 *www.boskerisshotel.co.uk* Two star hotel furnished in a modern style. 3 minutes uphill from the station.
TREGORRAN HOTEL - Tel: 01736 795889 *www.carbisbay.com* Modest hotel with Mediterannean feel. 5 minutes from station.
FAIRFIELD HOUSE - Tel: 01736 793771 *www.fairfield-house.net* Comfortable and friendly guest house accommodation overlooking sea about 4 minutes walk from the station.

Lelant

Pronounced as a Frenchman might say 'Le Lant', this was a busy market town and port in medieval times, the now isolated parish church of St Uny reflecting this lost prosperity. Early 17th century storms silted up the harbour, and the old town now lies submerged beneath the breezy links of the West Cornwall Golf Course.

Accommodation, Eating & Drinking
BADGER INN - Fore Street (4 minutes uphill from the station). Tel: 01736 752181 *www.badgerinnstives.co.uk* Virginia Woolf used to stay in this handsome stone-built pub in the village centre. Good food, St Austell ales and accommodation.

Shopping
Post office stores on main road.

Walking
South West Coast Path and St Michael's Way, a former pilgrim's route to St Michael's Mount, now waymarked (13 miles) with the traditional pilgrim's symbol of a scallop shell.

Lelant Saltings

Park and ride facility handily placed by A30 junction. Paradise Park Wildlife Sanctuary nearby - Tel: 01736 751020 *www.paradisepark.org.uk*

St Erth

St Erth was an Irish bishop who landed in this part of Cornwall in the 5th century. The village is located on the fringe of a former mining district which lends it a certain sombre quality. The bridge over the River Hayle has four arches, reflecting past breadth rather than present vigour.

Accommodation, Eating & Drinking
STAR INN - Church Street (village centre, 1 mile south of station). Tel: 01736 752068. CAMRA recommended village local of considerable charm. Nice archive photographs adorn the walls of this 17th century inn. Food, accommodation and a good choice of real ale including Sharp's redoubtable Doom Bar.

Shopping
Small post office store (Mace) in village centre.

Things to Do
CHENEY MILL FARM PARK - Tel: 01736 759555. Open daily Easter to October. 'A magic world of animals'.

Connections
TAXIS - Star Cars. Tel: 01736 754040.

St Ives

Half artist's retreat, half seaside resort - wholly enchanting - St Ives attracts an eclectic and cosmopolitan clientele, yet retains sufficient quantities of the traditional character of a Cornish fishing port; perhaps because - to a certain extent - that is what it continues to be. You can still see seine netting being carried out close inshore - and when they're not working the seine boats are rowed competitively for the sheer fun of it. Art is equally important to St Ives, and has been since the railway encouraged the first visitors in the last quarter of the 19th century. Whistler and Sickert visited and in 1939 an artists colony developed as Ben Nicholson drew inspiration from the naive works of the fisherman/painter Alfred Wallis.

Accommodation
PEDN-OLVA - Tel: 01736 796222 *www.smallandfriendly.co.uk* Comfortable, well-appointed two star hotel handily located between the station and the town and offering excellent views across the harbour and Porthminster sands.
TREGENNA CASTLE - Tel: 01736 795254 *www.tregenna-castle.co.uk* Famous former railway hotel now enjoying a new era as a hotel, golf course, leisure complex and centre for self-catering.
CORNERWAYS - Bethesda Place. Tel: 01736 796706 *www.cornerways-guesthouse-st-ives.com* Daphne Du Maurier once stayed in this comfortable guest house close to the Tate St Ives.
INTERNATIONAL BACKPACKERS - Gabriel Street. Tel: 01736 799444 *www.backpackers.co.uk* Budget price hostel accommodation in former Wesleyan Chapel School.

Eating & Drinking
PORTHMINSTER CAFE - Tel: 01736 795352 *www.porthminstercafe.co.u*k Beachside restaurant which has won the approval of Rick Stein, Tim Smit and now Michael Pearson. Consumate cooking, unrivalled location between the station and the sands. Choice of eating inside or alfresco.
ALBA - The Wharf. Tel: 01736 797222. Smart, award-winning restaurant belying its setting alongside the town's Salvation Army hostel. Breakfast, lunches and dinners with fine views of the harbour.
BLUE FISH - Norway Lane. Tel: 01736 794204. Seafood restaurant in a quiet(ish) backwater, appropriately housed in former fish net loft.

Shopping
Gift shops and galleries galore (as you might expect) but also some fine independent shops that you'll enjoy sniffing out.

Things to Do
TOURIST INFORMATION - Guildhall. Tel: 01736 796297 *www.go-cornwall.com*
TATE ST IVES - Portmeor Beach. Tel: 01736 796226 *www.tate.org.uk* Famous gallery in powerful modern building on site of former gas works bombed during World War II, a place of pilgrimage for all with an enthusiasm for contemporary art. Also provides access to Barbara Hepworth's studio and garden.
ST IVES MUSEUM - Wheal Dream. Tel: 01736 796005. Open Easter to October daily ex Sun. Homely little museum devoted to local life - mines, lifeboats, shipwrecks, fishing etc. Small collection of local railwayana including name and number plates of 5006 *Tregenna Castle* which was far too big an express engine to ever work into humble St Ives!
BOAT TRIPS - Tel: 01736 797328. Go and see what the seals make of *you!*

Walking
South West Coast Path. Historic town walk leaflets available from the TIC.

Connections
TAXIS - Ace Cars, Tel: 01736 797799.
BUSES- useful links along the north coast (where there never was a railway) to the likes of Zennor and St Just. Tel: 0870 608 2 608.
BICYCLE HIRE - Blazing Saddles. Tel: 01736 755493.

Information

Using This Guide

Nineteen 'one inch to one mile' maps portray the routes of the eight featured branch lines in Devon and Cornwall, commencing with Barnstaple in the north and ending with St Ives in the south. Each map is accompanied by a running commentary on matters historical, topographical and related to railway operation. Emphasis is given from the main line junction to the branch line terminus in each case, but details are equally relevant for journeys made in the opposite direction.

At the end of each section a Gazetteer gives details of most of the places served by trains on each line. The Gazetteer gives a brief, pithy, or even terse 'pen portrait' of each place together with itemised information on places to eat or drink or find accommodation, visitor centres, shopping, cycling, walking and bus or taxi services. Where accuracy is deemed essential in the planning of itineraries you are urged to contact the telephone number quoted or the local tourist Information Centre for up to date details.

Scheduled Services

Wessex Trains operate the majority of services over the routes described. By and large service levels on the routes covered in this guide are as frequent as they have ever been, and the relatively modern diesel units of Classes 150, 153 and 158 which operate most trains over these routes are comfortable and reliable.

Charter Trains

A number of tour companies offer excursions to West Country destinations, some of which may be steam-hauled. Amongst those who have recently offered such tours are:
Hertfordshire Rail Tours - Tel: 01438 718125 www.traintrips.co.uk
NENTA Train Tours - Tel: 01691 406152 www.nentatraintours.co.uk
Past-Time Rail - Tel: 0871 871 4119 www.past-timerail.co.uk

Pathfinder Tours - Tel: 01453 835414
www.toursatpathfinder.freeserve.co.uk
Very Special Trains - Tel: 01233 860939 www.veryspecialtrains.co.uk

Sleeper Trains

First Great Western operate the Night Rivera Sleeper service between London Paddington and a number of stations on the main line between Exeter and Penzance. For further details call 0845 7000 125.

Bicycles

Apart from long-distance services to Paignton and (on Summer Saturdays) to Newquay, the branchlines of Devon & Cornwall are operated by diesel units on which space for bicycles is very limited. There are two spaces for bike use, available on a first-come, first-served basis, and a ban on bikes on some commuter services into Exeter in the morning and out of that city in the evening. For more information download the 'Cycling By Train' leaflet on the Wessex Trains website (www.wessextrains.co.uk) or pick up a copy at any of the staffed stations in the two counties.

Tickets & Travelpasses

The following stations covered in this guide are staffed, and tickets should be bought from the Booking Office before boarding the train: Barnstaple, Exeter St.Davids, Exeter Central, Exmouth, Dawlish, Teignmouth, Newton Abbot, Torquay, Paignton, Plymouth, Liskeard, Looe, Par, Newquay*, Truro, St.Erth, Lelant Saltings^, Carbis Bay^, and St.Ives*^ (* - Travel Agent alongside station, ^ - Summer only, - Park & Ride fare only). Elsewhere tickets must be purchased from the conductor on the train. Apart from the long-distance services to Paignton and (on Summer Saturdays) to Newquay, all services are Standard Class only. There are Railrover tickets for Cornwall, Devon, and the entire South West region, plus Standard and Cheap Day Return fares (the latter available after 0930 Mondays-Fridays, anytime weekends, except on the St.Ives Bay Line in July and August). Where Cheap Day Returns are available, so too are Groupsave fares, where three or four people can travel for the price of two adults. For groups of ten or more travelling together there are special group rates, but with limited capacity these must be booked in advance - please phone 0870 9000 767. Anyone with disabilities or requiring assistance getting on or off trains should call 0845 300 0517 a few days before their journey.

Full ticket information, timetable downloads and train running information is available on the Wessex Trains website www.wessextrains.co.uk

Events and Leaflets

Through the Devon & Cornwall Rail Partnership a wide range of events are organised, from music trains to rail ale trails and guided walks. Full details can be found on www.carfreedaysout.com or by phoning 01752 233094. With Wessex Trains a wide range of 'Days Out' and 'Line Guide' leaflets are produced, and can be downloaded from the Wessex website, ordered through the post by calling 0870 900 2318, or picked up at any staffed station.

Useful Contacts

Wessex Trains operate the branchline services on all the 'Great Scenic Railways of Devon & Cornwall'. Customer Services (including lost property), telephone 0845 6000 880, or email customer.services@wessextrains.co.uk
Website: www.wessextrains.co.uk Telesales for advance ticket purchase: 0870 9000 2320.
National Rail Enquiries Service will answer all train times questions for the whole of the UK. 08457 48 49 50. www.nationalrail.co.uk
Devon & Cornwall Rail Partnership for branchline events and promotions. 01752 233094. www.carfreedaysout.com www.railaletrail.com
Rail Passengers Committee for the West of England, the independent consumer body. 0117 926 5703. info.western@railpassengers.org.uk www.railpassengers.org.uk/Western
North Devon Rail Users Group, the oldest and largest of the supporter groups. www.ndrailusers.freeuk.com
British Transport Police, if you see anything suspicious. 0800 40 50 40.
ImageRail run the St.Ives Bay Line Gallery and Shop at St.Erth station, where a wide range of prints and postcards depicting the 'Great Scenic' lines and localities in all their stunning scenic glory can be bought - along with this book, of course! www.imagerail.com

wessextrains

The franchise to operate local services throughout South West England plus the Portsmouth-Cardiff mainline was set up in October 2001. From the outset, Wessex Trains has set out to work enthusiastically with its Local Authority partners and a wide range of public and private sector organisations in order to deliver the best possible service to its passengers. Contrary to the view that branchlines are in decline, Wessex Trains has gone for growth and increased services wherever possible - and the reward has been passenger numbers rising faster than the national average. Based in Exeter, the company is able to be responsive to the region's needs, and believes in the benefits of local management and listening to all who have an interest in the rail service. Wessex Trains has warmly welcomed the 'Community Railways' initiative, and is looking to build on its already extensive community ties. In addition to sponsorship of local events and groups, events have been held to mark historic milestones (such as 'Barnstaple 150' pictured here), and staff have also very successfully entered the many town carnivals which add colour to the region. There are Line Working Groups for all the 'Great Scenic Railways of Devon & Cornwall', and station friends groups are being encouraged. In a broader sense, greater community involvement is fostered through the line naming and branding exercise. The posters which start each chapter in this book not only reflect back on the golden era of railway art and design, but also help convey that sense of character, individuality and identity which are at the heart of the branchlines' appeal. These and other 'Great Scenic' items are for sale on the website or from the St.Ives Bay Line Shop on St.Erth station. www.wessextrains.co.uk

As part of its commitment to the branchlines of Devon & Cornwall, in 2003 Wessex Trains completed a £2.5m refurbishment of its 25-strong two-coach 'class 150' fleet - including putting unique picture vinyls on the outsides to promote a range of destinations and tourist attractions, and naming the trains too. In 2004 the fleet of 15 one-coach 'class 153s' will similarly be refurbished. Look out for the six Devon & Cornwall 'Great Scenic Railway' class 153s, in black and gold livery, also the following class 150s which have local sponsors and names:

150230 'The Tamar Kingfisher' (Tamar Valley Tourist Association)
150232 'The Coastal Connection' (South West Coast Path)
150233 'The Lady Margaret of Looe Valley' (Caradon District Council)
150234 'The National Trust' (National Trust)
150236 East Devon's Heaven theme (East Devon District Council)
150238 'Exeter Explorer' (Exeter City Council)
150241 'The Tarka Belle' (North Devon Marketing Bureau)
150244 'The West Cornwall Experience' (Penwith District Council)
150248 'The Great Gardens of Cornwall' (Great Gardens of Cornwall)
150253 'The Exmouth Avocet' (Exmouth Town Council)
150261 'The Riviera Flyer' (Torbay Council)
150263 'The Castles of Cornwall' (English Heritage)
150265 'The Falmouth Flyer' (National Maritime Museum Cornwall)
150266 'The Whitley Wonder' (Paignton Zoo)

Established in 1991, the **Devon & Cornwall Rail Partnership** is the oldest and largest of the now 40+ strong field of Community Rail Partnerships. These bring together the various Local Authorities, rail industry players and community interest groups, in order to focus on promoting greater use of branchlines by residents and tourists alike. This is not just altruism - it is recognised that rail transport is vital to rural economies as well as to rural communities. The support of the Countryside Agency is central to the extensive programme of events and promotions that DCRP undertake from their base at Plymouth University. Notable successes have been the obtaining of grants to undertake station refurbishment on many of the lines, and the reintroduction of Sunday services on the Tamar valley and Maritime Lines. Music trains are a regular feature on the Tarka and Tamar Valley Lines in particular, and the Rail Ale

Trails now cover four lines and have proved very popular. Two new ventures for 2004 have been undertaken in conjunction with Wessex Trains, namely introducing a carnet (book of tickets) available for the Tamar Valley Line from shops in the neighbouring villages, and re-opening the Ticket Office at Looe - after a break of 35 years. www.carfreedaysout.com

Special thanks also to:

Cornwall County Council, who as lead partner in the 'Riviera Project' of Local Authorities in Cornwall have invested in modernising stations and station facilities to a degree rarely matched elsewhere. This includes all of the branchlines, with Falmouth, Looe, Newquay and St.Ives all receiving attention in 2004 alone. The St.Ives Bay Line upgrade and doubled weekday service on the Atlantic Coast Line in 2004 are testimony to the effectiveness of the partnership between the County Council, Wessex Trains and DCRP. www.cornwall.gov.uk

Devon County Council, who as lead partner in the 'ExeRail' partnership of Local Authorities in Devon have long supported the Tarka Line service and underpinned the refurbishment of the Avocet Line stations. In addition, the County Council runs the 'Dartmoor Sunday Rover', which each summer provides a Sunday service on the line to Okehampton along with extensive bus links over the moor and with the Tamar Valley Line. www.devon.gov.uk

North Devon Rail Users Group, set up in 1978 as an independent voice to promote the Tarka Line. Its 200 members from Devon and indeed around the world have seem some major changes in that time, but remain enthusiastically committed to getting the most out of North Devon's only rail link, and promoting its value to the communities along the line. www.ndrailusers.freeuk.com

Virgin Trains, who run daily year-round services to Paignton and Penzance, plus bring large numbers of holidaymakers down to Devon & Cornwall on Summer Saturdays. www.virgintrains.co.uk

Photographs

Front cover - main picture: foot crossing and old mine chimney between Calstock and Gunnislake on the Tamar Valley Line; *inset:* Calstock Viaduct, Tamar Valley Line.

Page 1: ivy-covered overbridge on the Looe Valley Line between Causeland and Sandplace.

Page 2 - upper left: early morning passengers on the Tarka Line at Umberleigh; *upper centre:* carriage window view of Porth Kidney Sands on the St Ives Bay line; *upper right:* departure from Falmouth Docks on the Maritime Line; *centre left:* Bere Alston on the Tamar Valley Line; *centre right:* the old station at Dartmouth; *lower left:* Saltash on the Tamar Valley Line; *lower centre:* bridge number, Yeoford, Tarka Line; *lower right:* Virgin Voyager at Torquay on the Riviera Line.

Page 4: trains crossing at Umberleigh on the Tarka Line.

Page 8: Eggesford Church on the Tarka Line.

Page 11: Junction Pool near Kings Nympton on the Tarka Line.

Page 16: three views of Lympstone on the Avocet Line.

Page 19: trains crossing at Topsham on the Avocet Line.

Page 23: views in the vicinity of Starcross on the Riviera Line.

Page 25: Voyager on the sea wall at Teignmouth, Riviera Line.

Page 27: station horticulture on the Riviera Line.

Page 29: beach hut heaven on the Paignton & Dartmouth Steam Railway at Goodrington Sands.

Page 35: Okletor Crossing on the Tamar Valley Line above Calstock.

Page 36: Tavy Viaduct on the Tamar Valley Line.

Page 37: dusk falls at Bere Ferrers on the Tamar Valley Line.

Page 40: Looe Valley scenes - *left:* Class 153 unit between Sandplace and Causeland; *upper right:* Coombe Junction; *lower right:* early morning at Sandplace.

Page 42: two views taken at Terras Crossing, East Looe River.

Page 43: the station and the fish quay at Looe.

Page 46: left: Treffry Viaduct; *right:* Luxulyan Valley foxgloves, Atlantic Coast Line.

Page 49 : china clay country, St Dennis, Atlantic Coast Line.

Page 53: crossing Carnon Viaduct on the Maritime Line.

Page 54: Falmouth's trio of stations at the end of the Maritime Line - *left:* Falmouth Docks; *upper right:* Falmouth Town; *lower right:* Penmere.

Page 58: St Ives Bay scenes - *upper left:* Lelant; *lower left:* Carbis Bay; *upper right:* Hayle Estuary; *lower right:* above Porth Kidney Sands.

Page 61: Roche on the Atlantic Coast Line.

Page 64: Perranwell on the Maritime Line.

This page: lower quadrants at St Blazey, Atlantic Coast Line.

Also by Michael Pearson

Iron Roads North of Leeds
ISBN 0 9545383 5 8
Iron Road to the Isles
ISBN 0 907864 87 2
Iron Road to the Highlands
ISBN 0 907864 93 7
Iron Road to Whisky Country
ISBN 0 907864 94 5
Iron Roads to the Far North & Kyle
ISBN 0907864 98 8
Railway Holiday in Scotland
ISBN 0 907864 90 2
Coming Up With the Goods
ISBN 0 907864 81 3
Me, My Morgan & The Midlands
ISBN 0 907864 95 3
Pearson's Canal Companions (9 vols)*
Tel: 01788 546692 for details

Acknowledgements

The author and publisher extend grateful thanks to Wessex Trains and the Devon & Cornwall Rail Partnership for their support in the preparation of this book, especially Andrew Griffiths (who engineered the whole project) and Richard Burningham. Special thanks to Eric Leslie for his evocative Arcadian illustration for page 3 and George *Gone With Regret* Behrend for insider information on the old GWR. Many thanks to Virgin Trains for comfortable travel facilities highly appreciated at the end of busy working days. Thank you to Chris Grove and Bill Bailey of the Tamar Belle, Felicity Cole of Newton Abbot Museum, Rachel Griffiths of ImageRail and Pat Cocking of St Erth. Thanks to Paul Salveson of ACORP for his continued support and networking. Multo grazie a Giampiero Logiudice e tutto nostro amicos a STIGE per loro totto bene lavoro. Thanks as always to Karen Tanguy for her work in front of and behind the scenes and to his family for putting up with Mr Pearson's absences in the demanding face of the false god of work.